PLEASURE IN E
STAGE ON
JOHN FREEMAN'S DIARY

PLEASURE IN ENGLISH

A graded course in English Language
in five stages followed by the O Level Stage

By J. R. C. Yglesias and I. M. Newnham

MASTERY OF ENGLISH

An academic course
graded in five stages

STAGE ONE

Pleasure
in English

J. R. C. YGLESIAS, B.A.
and
G. FIELDEN HUGHES

Headmaster, Queens County School, Wimbledon

ILLUSTRATED BY
E. ROWAN

LONGMAN

LONGMAN GROUP LIMITED
London

Associated companies, branches and representatives
throughout the world

© J. R. C. Yglesias and G. Fielden Hughes 1961

First published 1961
Seventh impression 1971

ISBN 0 582 21690 7

ACKNOWLEDGMENTS

We are indebted to the following for permission to quote copy-
right material:
Messrs J. M. Dent & Sons Ltd and E. P. Dutton & Co Inc New
York for an extract from *Chang* by Elizabeth Morse; Messrs
Ginn & Company Ltd for an extract from *The Cable Story* by
J. R. C. Yglesias; the Estate of the late Mrs Frieda Lawrence,
Messrs William Heinemann Ltd and The Viking Press Inc New
York for a verse from 'Snake' from *The Complete Poems of D. H.
Lawrence* (*Collected Poems*), copyright 1929 by Jonathan Cape
Ltd and Harrison Smith Inc, 1957 by F. L. Ravagli; the Literary
Executors of the late Dr Alfred Noyes for three verses from 'The
Highwayman'; and Miss Marion MacWilliam for her adaption
of 'Hans Brinker or The Silver Skates' by Mary Dodge from *May
we Recommend* Book I, published by Longman Group Limited.
The Tenniel illustration on page 24 is reproduced from *Alice in
Wonderland* by permission of Macmillan & Co Ltd.

We are grateful to *The Times* and to Mr Emrys Jones of Pen-
maenrhos for permission to reproduce the photographs which
appear on the cover.

Printed in Hong Kong by
Dai Nippon Printing Co (International) Ltd

The Contents of
John Freeman's Diary

Introduction

PLEASURE IN ENGLISH is a systematic series in five graded stages, with one book for each stage. It covers a five-year course in English Language for pupils in all types of Secondary Schools, and it is specifically designed for those who do not intend to enter a university. The standard of attainment can be measured, if desired, by local and regional external examinations in the fourth and fifth years. In particular, Stage Five reaches the standard and meets the requirements of the U.E.I., R.S.A., and similar fifth year examinations.

There is emphasis on 'The purposeful use of language in meaningful activities', with particular attention to oral expression and comprehension. Throughout the course there is scope for dramatic work in the classroom; for projects centred on newspapers and magazines; for lectures and discussions; for intensive reading; and for letter writing. The necessary grammar is presented in a sensible and realistic way, and the exercises cover a wide range of work while providing a careful grading and offering a choice to the pupil.

In treating the understanding and the use of English as a means of communication, we have deliberately avoided that separation which leads to whole chapters devoted exclusively to one particular branch (poetry, grammar, composition, etc.). Rather than this isolation, we have preferred to include these various aspects of language within the framework of the chapters themselves, thereby ensuring a greater degree of unity. At the same time, we have preserved an orderly and graded sequence within the structure of each book.

In the work in *Pleasure in English* the formal is linked with the informal so that pupils will respond to the challenge to attain 'a clear, easy, correct and unselfconscious use of their mother tongue'. It will help to stimulate those qualities of vitality, eagerness and enthusiasm which we all possess. At the same time detailed teaching methods and wordy explanations are excluded. The pupil can get the best of these books only with help and expert guidance. This rests in the hands of the staff. They determine the pace and decide where to follow through a project, where to omit an exercise. A chapter represents two weeks' work, apart from those devoted to revision.

STAGE ONE contains 25 chapters of which three are revision, and one chapter forms a complete *Radio Play*, 'The Silver Skates', specially written for classroom performance as a dramatized excerpt. It is the actual radio script as broadcast by the B.B.C. The narrative for each chapter is based on the events in the life of the Freeman family as reported in the diary of fourteen-year-old John Freeman. There are also a number of literary extracts of prose and poetry from writers of merit. In most chapters there is library work as well as suggestions for further reading from modern authors. There is a *Who's Who* and a *Little Dictionary* as well as an index.

To list the names of all the staff and pupils who have done so much work for us on this book is impossible. But we wish to pay particular tribute to the following schools and individuals who have so kindly assisted us:

Miss R. M. Campbell, Kidbrooke School.

Miss J. Holman and Mrs Whitehead, Campions School, Boreham Wood.

Mrs Reid, Marksbury Road School, Bristol.

Miss K.M. Thomas, Speedwell School, Kingswood, Bristol.

A. E. Crawford, The County Secondary School, Steyning.

E. John, Norton School, Letchworth.

Miss E. Knapton, Quarles Secondary Girls' School, Romford.

Miss B. H. N. Geary, The Training College, Brighton.

Miss Leevers, Corner Hall Secondary Girls' School, Hemel Hempstead.

Miss S. McKee, Portslade Secondary School for Girls.

Mrs S. Lock, Brislington Secondary School, Bristol.

J. R. C. YGLESIAS *and* G. FIELDEN HUGHES

John Freeman's room

JOHN FREEMAN'S DIARY

1

Moving House

I DO WISH grown-ups wouldn't cry! I quite expected Grandma's tears, but I was furious when my Mother started, too. Furious, because I felt sad myself at saying goodbye to Grandma and our London house, and then all those tears nearly set me off as well as my sister Angela.

Of course, Grandma always cries whether she's happy or sad and I really couldn't blame Mother yesterday. Anyhow, Angela and I managed not to cry and in a couple of hours we were both laughing and shouting with excitement in our new house in Summervale.

This is a marvellous town, only a dozen-or-so miles from Buckingham Palace, on the edge of a large common and not far from a magnificent park. And so different from our old street in London! Here it is clean and modern with grass and trees between the pavement and the road. We've up-to-date colour schemes in every room in the house, with central heating as well, and here Angela and I each have a room of our very own.

My bed is along one wall; opposite it are some bookshelves which are under the window, and there is a built-in cupboard where my model aeroplane kit can go. My father and mother had everything almost ready for us when we arrived, and soon my room was 'ship-shape' as my Father

9

calls it. He is always using this sort of expression; he was in the Royal Navy for years and years. Now he is the owner of a shop not far away in the old part of the town.

From my window I can just see the airport on the far side of the common which has a large pond that I must explore later. It's really like the country here, birds, trees, flowers and all the fresh air in the world! No sign of autumn yet although August ended yesterday. We are lucky. I only hope that I shall like my school here as much as my old one. I am still sad to have left my London school.

This diary of mine all began after my history master gave me a book called *Samuel Pepys in London*. It made me decide to keep a diary myself; not that I shall have plagues and fires to write about. I was going to read the bit about the 1665 plague this evening, but I am too exhausted and full of fish and chips.

1. Reading for Meaning
(a) Why was John Freeman furious with his mother yesterday?
(b) Did Grandma go to Summervale?
(c) What is meant by *all those tears nearly set me off*?
(d) In what ways does John find the streets of Summervale different from London?
(e) What is the meaning of *ship-shape*?
(f) What word does John use which has the same meaning as *modern*?
(g) What made John decide to keep a diary?
(h) Describe the view from John's window.
(i) Why didn't John read about the plague of 1665 last night?
(j) Suggest another title for this chapter.
(k) Explain *no sign of*, *exhausted*.
(l) How many years ago was 1665?

2. Detective Reading and Discussion

(a) In spite of no actual date for this entry, *Moving House*, can you prove that it was written on September 1st?

(b) Is John's bed under the window or opposite to it?

(c) Where would John be able to sail a model boat?

(d) What signs of real country does John notice in Summervale?

(e) What did the Freemans have for supper?

(f) How do you know that Samuel Pepys was alive in 1665?

(g) How do you know John was happy at his London school?

(h) What is the name of John Freeman's sister?

(i) Discuss what it is like to move house.

3. Reading for Pleasure

Read what a poet, Walter de la Mare, says about a home he loved.

The house of my first remembrance, the house that to my last hour on earth will seem home to me, stood in a small green hollow on the verge of a wide heath. Its five upper windows faced far eastwards towards the weather-cocked tower of a village which rambled down the steep inclination of a hill. And, walking in its grand old garden—oh, the crocuses, the wallflowers, the violets!—you could see in the evening the standing fields of corn, and the dark furrows where the evening star was stationed, and a little to the south, upon a crest, a rambling wood of fir-trees and bracken.

Read the above passage again carefully. Notice that Walter de la Mare chose beautiful words and sentences and avoided plain or ordinary ones. He wanted to make his writing as beautiful as his memories of the house. For example, he wrote *my last hour on earth* and not *death*. He wrote *verge* instead of *edge*.

FOR DISCUSSION

(a) How many other beautiful words and sentences can you find in the passage?

(b) We notice that everything the poet tells us has to do with the outside of the house. Say something about the inside of the house as you picture it.

(c) Imagine someone reading the passage aloud—an actor perhaps—while an orchestra plays music. When would the music swell out to match the voice?

(d) Give Walter de la Mare's passage a title.

4. Looking at Words

Ideas and pictures which spring to mind when you see or hear a word or group of words may be called *associations*, e.g. pond:

> *water   boats   sails   rowing   bathing*

Give four of your own ideas or associations for each of the following: bookshelves   Navy   airfields   birds   history

5. Understanding English: The Sentence

Look at these two sentences:

> The lion roars.   The wheel turns.

Now look at the three groups of words below which are *not* sentences:

a town in England   making a mistake   across the road

NOTICE THAT:

A sentence must contain a number of words which make complete sense. A sentence begins with a capital letter. A sentence ends with a full stop. Each sentence must contain a complete thought.

(a) Write one short sentence about each of the following:

London   August   Walter de la Mare   Ice-cream

(b) Say which of the following are sentences:

The dog barks.	A new T.V. set
With a silly grin	I want an ice-cream.
He was absent.	Into the goal
John Freeman's diary	We must leave now.

(c) Write ten sentences about one of the following:

A journey to Outer Space   Washing-up   Christmas

6. Tricky Words

Write each of the following words in a separate sentence:

where   which   why   whisper   whistle   whole

Underline these words and learn to spell them.

7. Dictionary Work

Look up the meaning of each of the following words in your LITTLE DICTIONARY at the back of this book:

ignorance   furrows   avoid   swell   tragic

Write each of them in a separate sentence.

8. Describe what you see in the picture of John Freeman's room at the beginning of this chapter. Can you see anything which John Freeman has *not* mentioned in his diary?

9. Things to Do and Research Work

(a) Look up Walter de la Mare in your WHO'S WHO at the back of this book.

(b) Find and read the passages in Charles Dickens' book, *David Copperfield*, which describe David's bedroom and Mr Peggotty's house (Chapter 3).

(c) Find out if there is a copy of *Oliver Twist* in your school, and say who wrote it.

(d) Find out about Samuel Pepys from your WHO'S WHO.

(e) Find out the name and height of the highest mountain in Scotland.

2

Out and About

TODAY ANGELA and I spent a busy morning helping in the house. Father was down at his new shop in Fore Street so I was put in charge of the bathroom lino. Apparently it was laid some months ago, so it had stretched and all I had to do was to trim the edges and tack it down. Apart from hitting my head twice, once on the bath, once on the basin, and banging my right thumb with the hammer, everything went smoothly.

Angela fixed the lamp shades and swept out the hall. She was singing away merrily all the morning. Perhaps she'll end up as a famous singer. Everyone says she has a fine voice and she's not bad-looking either. At the moment she is aiming to grow her hair into a pony tail but Mother insists on plaits.

In the afternoon I put on my new jeans and took my model aeroplane out for a trial on the common. There was rather too much wind at first, but I managed some excellent flights later.

At one point my plane landed in the pond and I had a quarrel with another boy there. Afterwards I was told that he lives near us and is called Jenkins. A pretty tough customer, I fear, but not popular with the others round the pond who took my side.

Fortunately the ice-cream van rang its bells and this prevented a stand-up fight as Jenkins ran off to buy one and left us in peace. Then I was late home, but no serious trouble as Mother doesn't expect us to know our way around yet.

I'm sure I will never be able to write such an interesting diary as Samuel Pepys, but tomorrow Angela and I go to our new schools and *that* event will certainly be recorded in JOHN FREEMAN'S DIARY! I wonder what school will be like in Summervale?

1. Reading for Meaning

(a) Why was there so much to do in the Freeman house this morning?

(b) Why didn't Mr Freeman tack down the lino?

(c) What does John mean by *perhaps she'll end up as a famous singer*?

(d) Apart from her lovely voice, what other advantage has Angela which might help her to become a famous singer?

(e) What is meant by *a pretty tough customer*?

(f) What is meant by *a stand-up fight*?

(g) What prevented a stand-up fight with Jenkins?

(h) Suggest another title for this chapter.

2. Detective Reading and Discussion

(a) How do you know that John Freeman is left-handed?

(b) Why was the bathroom lino not tacked down when it was first laid months ago?

(c) What wood is used for a model aeroplane?

(d) Explain how to fix a lamp shade to an electric light.

(e) How do you know that neither Angela's junior school nor John's secondary school have started the new term yet?

(f) Pony tail or plaits? Discuss which you prefer for a ten-year-old girl.

(g) Suggest the work that Mrs Freeman was probably doing this morning in the new house.

(h) What are 'jeans'?

(i) Is it necessary for a singer to have good looks?

(j) What differences are there between living in a town and living in the country?

3. Looking at Words

(a) Give your own ideas or associations for:

ice-cream   aeroplane   sweet-shop   cupboard   doctor

(b) Imagine you are on Summervale Common when there is a firework display. Give a list of things you see, e.g. trees, leaves, shadows, grass, and so on. Make your list as complete as you can as the fireworks light up the scene.

(c) Give ten separate sentences, each containing one word from your own list for (b) above.

4. Reading for Pleasure

> I remember, I remember,
> The house where I was born,
> The little window where the sun
> Came peeping in at morn;
> He never came a wink too soon,
> Nor brought too long a day,
> But now, I often wish the night
> Had borne my breath away.
>
> I remember, I remember
> The roses, red and white,
> The violets and the lily-cups—
> Those flowers made of light!
> The lilacs where the robin built,
> And where my brother set
> The laburnum on his birthday—
> The tree is living yet!

I remember, I remember
Where I used to swing,
And thought the air must rush as fresh
To swallows on the wing;
My spirit flew in feathers then
That is so heavy now,
And summer pools could hardly cool
The fever on my brow.

I remember, I remember
The fir trees dark and high;
I used to think their slender tops
Were close against the sky.
It was a childish ignorance,
But now 'tis little joy
To know I'm farther off from Heaven
Than when I was a boy.

FOR DISCUSSION

(a) How can you tell that Thomas Hood, who wrote this poem,
preferred the past to the present?

(b) What other flowers besides those mentioned in the verse
would you like in your own garden?

(c) Say which particular lines you find the most pleasing.

5. Punctuation: Full Stops and Commas.

Look at the punctuation marks in these sentences:

One day, as I was walking home, I met my mother. Her bag
was loaded with eggs, apples, cheese and soap powder.

The word *punctuation* means pointing or putting points or
marks among words in a piece of writing. When is it necessary
to punctuate with a full stop?

A comma (,) is used to show a short pause in reading:

One fine day, as I was walking home, I met my mother.

B

A comma is also used to separate words in a list:

> Her shopping bag was loaded with eggs, apples, cheese and soap powder.

Here are three guides to help you to punctuate correctly:

Put a full stop at the end of every complete sentence.

Put a comma to show a short pause in reading.

Put a comma to separate words in a list.

Look again at the sentences at the beginning of this exercise. Notice that there is no comma before the word *and*. You will find some writers put commas before words such as *and*, *but*, *so*.

Put the full stops and commas in the following passage. Remember to start every sentence with a capital letter.

> Last week when on the journey to Summervale John and Angela saw a large common John noticed the trees the birds the pond and the airfield that evening he arranged his aeroplane kit his stamp album and railway rolling stock in the cupboard in his bedroom Angela noticed on her way upstairs that the light was still on in John's room he was writing his diary tomorrow Angela and John Freeman start at their new schools in Summervale

6. Dictionary Work

Look up the meaning of each of the following words in your LITTLE DICTIONARY at the back of this book:

> quaint   saddler   jumbled   infectious

Write each of them in a separate sentence of your own.

7. Things to Do and Library Work

(a) Make a list of your six favourite books.

(b) Can you name the six authors of the books on your list?

(c) Read a book from one of your friends' lists.

(d) Look up Thomas Hood in your WHO'S WHO.

3

New Schools in Summervale

ANGELA AND I discussed the first day at our new school this evening. One thing struck us both immediately. In London we had to walk for fifteen minutes from the school to a park for games. But here in Summervale, both at Angela's Junior School and my Secondary School, the playing fields are at the doorstep, with shower baths laid on in the changing rooms.

Angela is ten and I left her at the gate of her school and went on to my school further down the road. As a matter of fact, I felt like a fish out of water when I first crossed the playground there this morning.

By the end of the afternoon both of us found we were thoroughly at home. They all knew about Angela, and several girls asked about her singing. Apparently the headmistress there had told them about Angela Freeman, a promising newcomer for the school choir.

I was a bit lost for a few minutes, then the headmaster himself spotted me and put me at my ease at once. He is tall, with very broad shoulders and what is called 'an infectious grin', the sort of smile that is catching. He took me to my form room and introduced me to my form-master. Like Angela, I was then given the necessary exercise and text books.

Angela said she was too excited to learn a great deal in the morning. Much the same happened to me. I sat next to

Charlie Hunter and during break he told me his father is the choirmaster at Summervale Church. I hear there is some kind of school choirs festival there soon. I hope that Angela, Charlie and I will all be singing.

A great deal more than I have written here happened to us on this first day at our new schools. I am sure Samuel Pepys must have had more time than I have to keep his diary up to date. I have already given up the idea of keeping a *daily* record and shall content myself with short accounts of specially interesting things that happen to me and my family. After all, Samuel Pepys was grown-up. I am only fourteen years old.

1. Reading for Meaning

(a) What exactly does John Freeman mean by. *One thing struck us both immediately*?

(b) How long did it take John to walk from school to the games field in London?

(c) What expression does John use to show he felt strange when he entered his new school?

(d) How old is Angela Freeman?

(e) Who first spotted John Freeman?

(f) Discuss John's words, *an infectious grin* and *a smile that is catching*.

(g) Who sat next to John Freeman in class?

(h) Who is the choirmaster at Summervale Church?

(i) How old is John Freeman?

(j) What has John decided about the keeping of his diary in the future?

(k) Explain the meaning of each of these words as used in the above passage:

      newcomer   introduced   break   festival
      accounts   record   content   grown-up

(l) Suggest another title for this chapter.

2. Detective Reading and Discussion

(a) What are the advantages of having playing fields at the school doorstep?

(b) Who could have told the headmistress that Angela was a good singer?

(c) What time do you think Pepys had for writing his diary that John has not?

(d) How do you know that John Freeman's headmaster was a kindly man?

(e) At what age do you think a person is grown-up?

3. Looking at Words

Give your associations, or picture-words for:

      choir   playground   diary   grown-ups   classroom

4. Reading for Pleasure

James Woodforde was born in 1740 and died in 1803. He was a clergyman and he kept a diary which has become famous. Its title is *The Diary of a Country Parson*. Like all diaries, it gives us a picture of the times in which it was written. Even more important, it shows us the kind of person the writer was.

Here is Mr Woodforde's entry for one day. It is a little picture of the times in which he lived. Read it carefully.

August 11*th*, 1788

Mr Walker and Betsy Davy came over on single Horses this morning from Foulsham and they breakfasted, dined, and spent the Afternoon with us. We had a good deal of singing to Day from my Niece and Mr Walker—the latter sung many new Songs. We spent a very agreeable Day together. We had for Dinner a boiled Leg of Mutton and Capers, a Couple of rost Chicken, Apple Pie and black Currant Tarts—Apricots, Apples and black Currants for Desert. Mr Walker and Betsy Davy came to us about

9 o'clock this morning and stayed till half past six in the evening. We had a note that Mr and Mrs Bodham would dine here on Wedn.

FOR DISCUSSION

(a) What is meant by *single* horses?

(b) The guests came early and went early. Why?

(c) What two pleasures of the day did Mr Woodforde most enjoy?

(d) Mr. Woodforde sometimes felt unwell. Can you suggest any reasons for this?

(e) What sauce did they have with the meat course?

(f) Which words would not have capital letters in modern English today?

(g) What abbreviation is used for *Wednesday*?

5. Understanding English—Subject and Predicate

Look at these sentences. *The lion roars. The wheel turns.* They each have two parts:

THE PERSON OR THING NAMED	WHAT IS TOLD ABOUT THE PERSON OR THING
The lion	roars
The wheel	turns

These two parts of a sentence are called:

THE SUBJECT	and	THE PREDICATE
The lion		roars
The wheel		turns

Notice the subjects underlined below and remember that the rest of the sentence is the predicate.

Charlie heard the birds singing in the trees.

Down the aisle came the bride.

Every day we eat breakfast.

Who has seen Hunter?

It was cold and dark.

(a) Pick out the subjects in the following sentences:

He was never absent.	Angela likes ice-cream.
Away flew my cap.	They found my bicycle.
She found her brooch.	Charlie is swimming.
Hunter broke his pencil.	Near the fire sat the dog.

(b) Pick out the predicates in each sentence above.

6. Look at these two sentences:

> We went out.   The sun was shining.

They can be joined to make a single sentence:

> We went out *because* the sun was shining.

Use each of the following words once only to make single sentences from each of the pairs below.

> *but   that   when   which   and   where   because*

There were some boxes.	We used for chairs.
They were so small.	I could have crushed them.
The candle flickered.	It did not go out.
We went to bed.	It was dark.
We reached Summervale.	We went to bed.
We sat down.	The grass was dry.

Look at the first sentence which begins at line 8 on page 19. Notice that here three sentences are all joined to make a single sentence beginning with a capital letter and ending with a full stop. Here the joining word *and* is used twice.

7. Tricky Words

Write each of the following words in a separate sentence:

> always   almost   alone   already   also   although

Underline the above words in your sentences and make sure you can spell them.

8. Alphabetical Order

Arrange these words in strict alphabetical order:

either	neither	whisper	friend	whole
receive	why	believe	draper	nine

9. Things to Do

(a) Find out if it is possible for you to hear some of the following passages read aloud:

The passage in *Tom Brown's Schooldays* by Thomas Hughes which describes a tea-party in the school house (Chapter 6).

The passage in Charlotte Brontë's *Jane Eyre* which describes breakfast in a girls' school (Chapter 5).

The Mad Hatter's Tea Party in *Alice in Wonderland* by Lewis Carroll (Chapter 7).

(b) Write down the names of three characters you have met and liked in books and name the books and the authors.

(c) What scene does the picture below show? In what book would you expect to find it?

A well-known picture from a famous book

4

Our Shop

AFTER SCHOOL today my sister Angela and I went along to my father's new shop. When he was a young man he served in the Royal Navy. At the end of his service he bought a shop in Camberwell where he sold sweets and tobacco.

We moved from Camberwell because he bought this new shop in Summervale. It stands in Fore Street, which is really the centre of the old village of Summervale. The new town is built all around it. This old-fashioned street winds its way along between shops and houses more like a river than the busy road which it has now become. It is lined on both sides by shady trees.

There are no supermarkets or stores in Fore Street. The shops are all owned and managed by local tradesmen with their own names on boards above the windows. Some of them have the date when the business was started, like this: WM. WILSON: DRAPER. ESTABLISHED 1873.

My father's shop is in the front downstairs room of a Georgian house. The upstairs rooms are let as a flat to Charlie Hunter's family and for this reason we cannot live over the shop. I don't mind this, because I would much rather live in our new house.

At the door of our shop stands an object which my father brought with him from Camberwell and which he values highly. It is a life-size figure of a sailor in the uniform worn in the Royal Navy in the nineteenth century.

My father bought the Bo'sun, as he calls it, at a marine store in Chatham. It may have been a ship's figurehead or perhaps part of a museum group.

The Bo'sun stands just outside the door, on the left-hand side, looking (I think) rather fiercely at the customers, as if he would take his cutlass to them if they were not very careful how they behaved.

The front of Mr Freeman's shop

Just inside the door is a tall stand with walking sticks in it. I don't think we sell many, but most shops like ours have them. The shelves are all neat and tidy. Along the top shelf are large jars full of every kind and variety of sweets from mint humbugs to jelly babies. Below is the chocolate shelf, all boxes, and on the counter itself are the many different makes of slab chocolate.

Cigarettes, tobacco and cigars are stored on the lowest shelf on a level with the counter. There is also a glass case containing lighters, cigarette holders and ash trays. These are all carefully marked with a price tag.

Opposite the counter is the chief centre of attraction: the

refrigerator loaded with delicious ice-creams! Above it hangs a cage with a pair of blue budgerigars in it.

1. Reading for Meaning

Here are the *answers* to certain questions which Charlie Hunter asked John Freeman about this chapter of his diary.

You have to write down the *questions* to which they are the answers:

> e.g. John Freeman went to his father's shop.
> *Question:* Where did John go after school?

(a) He served for some years in the Royal Navy.

(b) He took a shop at Camberwell when he retired.

(c) Summervale is a new town built round an old village.

(d) It winds its way along like a river.

(e) Charlie Hunter's family live there.

(f) He bought the Bo'sun in Chatham.

(g) The large jars are on the top shelf.

(h) It is opposite the counter.

(i) There are budgerigars in it.

(j) There are lighters, cigarette holders and ash trays in it.

2. Detective Reading and Discussion

(a) What provides some shade for shoppers in Fore Street?

(b) How many shops in Fore Street, Summervale, have branches in Liverpool and Manchester?

(c) What does Wm. stand for?

(d) Describe the contents of a draper's shop.

(e) Consider the use of the word *winds* in the sentence, *this old-fashioned street winds its way along*.

(f) For how many years have the Wilson family been drapers?

(g) What is a marine store?

(h) Is the Bo'sun over three feet high?

(i) What date was it half-way through the nineteenth century?

(j) What shops sell walking-sticks?

(k) What is ice-cream made of?

(l) Suggest another title for this chapter.

(m) Explain the meaning of *life size* and *slab chocolate.*

3. Looking at Sentences

Look at this sentence about Fore Street:

> This old-fashioned street winds its way along between shops and houses more like a river than the busy road which it has become.

If Fore Street really was a waterway and not a road, it might make you think of a certain Italian city.

(a) Can you make up five sentences about a city whose streets are waterways, and name it?

John Freeman tells us about the shopkeepers in Fore Street with names and dates on boards above the windows. His father's shop is in a Georgian house, which means that it must be at least a hundred and fifty years old.

(b) Write not more than ten sentences about the old-fashioned Fore Street of Summervale as it must have appeared in the eighteenth century using some of these words and their associations: wigs knee-breeches buckled shoes horses

4. Reading for Pleasure

Read this short description of Venice from *Journey into a Picture* by Mary Bosanquet.

... suddenly we were in Venice. It was all dancing and glimmering around us: houses, churches and palaces stippled with light and shadow, their walls netted with the flickering patterns of the sea's face which was dimpling in the sun. Nothing kept still, houses, churches, palaces, everything rippled, bathed clear in the mingled brightness of water and sky. And silent as snakes the black and sinuous gondolas went sliding through the silver veins of the city. We slipped along the Grand Canal past many palaces, delicate and strange, whose great carved doorways opened into the sea, and whose arched windows winked back the light splashed up from the water.

FOR DISCUSSION

Which words and sentences do you consider to be unusual and colourful?

Suggest a new title for this passage:

What does a gondola look like?

In what way are canals in England different from those in Venice?

5. Punctuation: Full stops, question marks, exclamation marks.

(a) One morning a recruit was crossing the parade ground when he met the Sergeant-Major, a fierce-looking man with a large moustache. The conversation below took place between them.

It is made up of questions, statements, commands and exclamations. Decide which of these each line of conversation is, then copy out and punctuate the whole passage.

For a statement   —put a full stop   (.)
For a question   —put a question mark   (?)
For a command   —put an exclamation mark   (!)
For an exclamation—put an exclamation mark   (!)

Decide who spoke first, the Sergeant-Major (put s) or the Private (put P), and write the correct letters at the beginning of each line all the way through.

Halt

Sir

Who are you

The name is Smith

General Smith

Oh no Private Smith

How dare you go about with your collar undone

I'm not properly dressed yet

That's what I'm saying

I mean I'm not on parade
On the parade ground you are always on parade
I didn't know that
And what on earth
I beg your pardon
What is that round your neck
A silk handkerchief
Good heavens
I suffer from the cold
Take it off
I suffer from the cold
Do not repeat yourself
I thought you did not hear
Listen
Yes sir
Take off that — muffler and button up your tunic
Sir
At once
Certainly sir
In future remember you are a soldier
I will sir
And never let me see you like that again

(b) Refer to excercise 5 in Chapter 2 and read the three guides
to help you punctuate (p. 18). Now study these two sentences:

Take it off!   Who are you?

NOTICE:

If the sentence is asking a question, always put a question
mark. *It takes the place of a full stop.*
e.g. Who are you? How was that done? Where are you
going?

An exclamation mark is used after words and sentences
which give an order or show some sudden feeling which
would make us raise our voices a little.

e.g.: Take it off! How strange! Oh! Hullo! Remember you are a soldier!

(c) Punctuate the following passage putting in all the full stops, commas and question marks, as well as one exclamation mark to show sudden feeling.

Last night there was a knock at our back door about ten o'clock who do you suppose it was nobody was more astonished than my mother she opened the door and saw it was my uncle Fred who went to Australia twenty years ago none of the family had seen him since then and of course we children had never seen him at all he was a short man with grey hair blue eyes and a very sunburnt face how do you think he had travelled from Melbourne to London he had done it in a small boat all by himself next day the papers were full of his trip when he saw the accounts what do you suppose he said he merely remarked very quietly that he could not understand what all the fuss was about but then Uncle Fred was never a one to boast

6. Tricky Words

Write each of the following words in a separate sentence:

knob   comb   calm   island   listen

Each one has a *silent letter*—which is it?

Underline these words in your sentences and make sure you can spell them.

Now do the same with:

believe   niece   chief   piece   friend

7. Dictionary Work

Look up the meaning of each of these words in your LITTLE DICTIONARY at the back of this book:

gondola   weary   precious   tunic   mingle
jealous   delicate   emigrate   draper

8. Joining Sentences

(a) Write sentences using the joining words:

and   where   because   but

(b) Make up a story as though Bo'sun were a sailor in an old sailing ship caught in a storm. Let Bo'sun tell the story.

9. Things to Do

Read the first chapter of *Little Women* by Louisa May Alcott, and write down one fact about each of the four sisters.

Write down four sentences about Angela Freeman and four sentences about Charlie Hunter.

State the advantages and disadvantages about one of the following as a pet:

a dog	a cat	white mice	a tortoise
a budgerigar	a pony	a monkey	a rabbit

10. Any Answers?

(a) Who is the Prime Minister?

(b) Who is Leader of the Opposition?

(c) Who is your local M.P.?

Name this famous building and the clock

5

Bullets in the Church

TONIGHT MY SISTER Angela and I went to our first choir practice in the new church at Summervale.

Although I say *new* church, I only mean new to us. In fact it is a very old church, with its lych-gate at the end of Fore Street. We went through this gate and across the church-yard with its long grass, old tomb-stones and tall trees. Then we entered the church by the south door.

The old church in Summervale

A part of the church was built in Norman times, but most of it is fifteenth century. Angela says you can tell which is which, because the Norman part has semi-circular arches and very thick pillars and the stones of the pillars are not very close together, because the mortar is rather thick between them.

Angela told me that the main point to notice about a Norman building is the semi-circular arches, usually a sign that the Normans built it. She says that they did not know how to make pointed arches for some time, so the Norman part of our church is probably twelfth century work. I know very little about church buildings myself but Angela is doing some work on the Normans at school, and she is especially interested in old buildings. Her other main interest is music, and she has a lovely voice. She might be chosen for the solo part when we sing 'On Wings of Song' at the Festival.

Our new choirmaster is my friend Charlie Hunter's father and he took us round the church after choir practice. He led us to the south door and pointed out five holes in it large enough to put your finger-tip into quite easily.

'They're bullet holes,' he said. 'They were made by the Roundheads, Cromwell's men. A Cavalier—one of King Charles I's followers—rushed into the church for sanctuary. But the Roundheads had no respect for that ancient custom, so they shot at him. These are the bullet holes. The Cavalier banged the door behind him and the shots went into this door. Now come and see the actual bullets.'

Mr Hunter then showed us the bullets, taken out of the door and put in a glass case. They were old-fashioned, badly-shaped leaden balls. It all made me alter my opinion about 'the good old days'. Angela, of course, was far more intelligent about all this than I was. She is going to read an account of those exciting times in a book which Mr Hunter has lent her. Frankly, I was rather bored, but perhaps I was really a bit jealous of my sister's knowledge. Anyhow, I'm not jealous of her singing and I do hope she does well in the tests for the solo part next week.

1. Reading for Meaning

(a) Where did Angela and John Freeman go for their first choir practice?

(b) Why were the stones of the pillars not very close together?

(c) Who is doing some work on the Normans at school?

(d) How big were the five bullet holes?

(e) Where were the actual bullets kept?

(f) What name is given to one of King Charles I's followers?

(g) Who showed the Freemans round the church?

(h) What is another way of saying, *It made me alter my opinion*?

(i) What name is given to Cromwell's men?

(j) When are the tests for the solo part in *On the Wings of Song* to be held?

(k) Suggest another title for this chapter.

(l) Explain the meaning of *bored jealous intelligent solo*.

2. Detective Reading and Discussion

(a) Imagine you are showing someone round Summervale church. Explain how you can tell that parts of it were built in Norman times.

(b) When John Freeman stood inside the south door of the church, on one hand would be the altar, on the other the ropes hanging down from the belfry. Which was on his left and which on his right?

(c) How could John tell that the bullet holes in the door were not made in modern times?

(d) Why does Angela know more about Norman churches than her brother?

(e) What song will the choir and soloist sing at the church Festival?

(f) Do you think John was really jealous of his sister?

(g) Discuss the meaning of the word 'sanctuary' as used in this chapter.

(h) What date was it half-way through the fifteenth century?

3. Looking at Words

Give six other words or associations that spring to your mind for each of the following:

> choir   tomb-stones   Norman   bullet   pulpit

4. Reading for Pleasure

The little, dancing river by whose grassy banks we had eaten our welcome lunch had followed our swift steps with a swifter flow of its own, and had come to the tall, black rock which made the waterfall. Over came the gleaming water, breaking into a silvery sweep, throwing up a glittering spray made golden by the hot and brilliant sun. Our hearts were filled with a leaping delight like a lovely reflection of the singing, rushing water. The roaring sound as it fell, the glassy curve of the frothing pool below, the flying spray touching our sunburnt cheeks with its cool fingers, the fresh smell of the bracken, all combined to give us an exciting feeling, as if we must burst into loud song.

FOR DISCUSSION

(a) See how many vivid words and sentences you can find in the above passage.

(b) Give this passage a title.

(c) What sound and sights do you associate with *ocean* waves?

(d) Would the above description be suitable for the River Thames? Give reasons.

5. Understanding English: Four Kinds of Sentences

(a) Look at the five sentences printed at the bottom of page 22 in Chapter 3. Notice that four of these are statements and one is a question.

(b) When we talk, we may give orders (commands). The Sergeant-Major, that fierce-looking man with a moustache in

Exercise 5, Chapter 4, certainly gives commands. Check his words (pp. 29–30).

You have already met three kinds of sentences:

STATEMENT: It was cold and dark.

QUESTION: Who has seen Hunter?

COMMAND: Take it off!

Look at this sentence: *Put your books away!* Can you find the subject? In the case of commands (or orders) the subject is often not spoken or written. For example, in the sentence, *Put your books away!* the subject of the sentence is YOU, who are told to put the books away. But the word YOU is *understood* to come before the first word and is not written or spoken: (you) Put your books away!

(a) Say which of the following sentences are statements, questions or commands:

> Come and help me with my work.
> Why must dogs howl at the moon?
> Where shall we go for our holiday?
> Do not alight till the bus stops.
> The clock has stopped.
> Send it to the clock-maker.
> Last night the moon had a golden ring.
> Charge the guns!
> There lay the missing sixpence.
> Who lost it?
> Never a word spoke she.

(b) Now write down the above sentences and underline the subject in each. (Supply one if it is *understood*.)

There is one other kind of sentence: EXCLAMATION.
e.g. How well I feel! You are an idiot!

(c) Write four sentences according to the following plan:
The *question* your father asked you when you came home late with muddy shoes on.

The *statement* you gave in reply.

The *command* your father gave you about your muddy shoes.

The *exclamation* you made under your breath.

6. Tricky Words

Write each of the following words in a separate sentence:

should   fourth   round   colour   would   house

Underline the words in your sentences and make sure you can spell them.

7. Dictionary Work

Look up the meaning of each of these words in your LITTLE DICTIONARY at the back of this book:

solo   sanctuary   chancel   pulpit   lych-gate
mortar   narrative

8. Written Work

Describe shortly how to look after and feed any animal or pet which you know about.

9. Things to Do and Library Work

(a) Can you tell a story connected with three of the following?
Just William   Lochinvar   Jennings   Aladdin   Heidi
The Pied Piper of Hamelin

(b) Look up *Roundheads* and *Cavaliers* in an encyclopaedia.

(c) Check the Tricky Words in Exercise 6, Chapter I, and make sure you can still spell them correctly.

(d) What event do you associate with *The Little Town of Bethlehem*?

(e) Name three towns in England, one in Scotland and one in Wales where there is a cathedral.

(f) In what book is the story of the Creation written?

6

A Visit from the Police

I THINK ANGELA has lost the chance of singing the solo part in the church Festival. Charlie Hunter's father, the choirmaster, is furious with her because she was late for the tests yesterday. And all because of the police!

I suppose Angela did not like to tell Mr Hunter that she was late because she had to go to the police station. Not that *she* had done anything wrong. But it was a bit awkward. A policeman came to our house to enquire about some shop-lifting at our sweet and tobacco shop in Fore Street. Apparently Angela saw some suspicious characters when she was there and the police wanted her to tell them all about it.

So by the time they had finished questioning her, she was late reaching the church for the singing tests. She was too shy to tell Mr Hunter in front of the whole choir what had happened. I could not think what had happened, but when she told me afterwards, I was furious with her and with Mr Hunter. I think I will have a word with Charlie at school tomorrow and ask him to tell his father exactly why Angela was late.

Another thing made me furious. Our neighbours saw the police call at our house and started gossiping. Later, young George Jenkins began to shout at me saying that our family was in trouble with the police. That started it. I told him he was probably the shop-lifting expert the police were looking for. This made him attack me, as I hoped, and we had a real set-to in the street. Up went the windows, and the other kids gathered round and there was quite a scene.

George and I were hauled off home by our mothers, but not before we had given each other quite a few knocks. Now I'm furious with him, my mother, Angela, Mr Hunter and with the entire police force! No doubt I will be adding my father to the list shortly after he comes home! I know he will be pretty angry with *me* when he hears about my street fight!

But I must get a message through to Mr Hunter about Angela being late for the solo test for *On Wings of Song*.

I suppose George Jenkins and I will soon be friendly again once the real truth about the police visit is known in our street.

The police car outside the Freeman's house

1. Reading for Meaning

(a) Why was Angela late for the solo tests yesterday?

(b) Give the surname of the choirmaster and the Christian name of his son.

(c) Why did a policeman call at the Freeman's house?

(d) Why was John furious with George Jenkins?

(e) Who else made John furious and why?

(f) Who stopped the street fight?

(g) Why does John use the word *apparently* in the sentence, *Apparently Angela saw some suspicious characters*?

(h) Suggest another title for this chapter.

(i) Explain the meaning of *gossip*, *entire*, *visit*.

2. Detective Reading and Discussion

(a) Was Mr Hunter right to be furious with Angela?

(b) If you had been Angela, what would you have done?

(c) What sort of things do *you* gossip about?

(d) Give an account of the conversation between John and his father yesterday evening.

(e) How would a message to Charlie help Angela Freeman?

(f) What song was taken for the solo test?

(g) What has happened to Angela's hair? See p. 14, lines 13–14, and the picture opposite.

3. Reading for Pleasure

Here are the first three verses of a poem by Alfred Noyes called *The Highwayman*.

The wind was a torrent of darkness among the gusty trees,
The moon was a ghostly galleon tossed upon cloudy seas,
The road was a ribbon of moonlight over the purple moor,
And the highwayman came riding—
    Riding—riding—
The highwayman came riding, up to the old inn-door.

He'd a French cocked hat on his forehead, a bunch of lace at
     his chin,
A coat of scarlet velvet, and breeches of brown doe-skin.
They fitted with never a wrinkle. His boots were up to the thigh,
And he rode with a jewelled twinkle,
     His pistol butts a-twinkle,
His rapier hilt a-twinkle, under the jewelled sky.

Over the cobbles he clattered and clashed in the dark inn-yard.
And he tapped with his whip on the shutter, but all was locked
     and barred.
He whistled a tune to the window, and who should be waiting
     there
But the landlord's black-eyed daughter,
     Bess, the landlord's daughter,
Plaiting a dark red love-knot into her long black hair.

FOR DISCUSSION
(a) How has the poet made his description of the wind, the
    moon and the road seem so effective?
(b) How is it you can almost *hear* the highwayman riding up to
    the old inn-door?
(c) What is the difference between poetry and prose?
(d) Why is this poem called a *narrative* poem?

4. Looking at Words

Give the associations suggested by three of the following:
    gondola   spray   fir-trees   violets
    galleon   ghostly   cobbles   moonlight

5. Understanding English: Paragraphs

Examine John Freeman's diary at the beginning of this chapter,
A visit from the police, and notice that in lines 5, 13 and 21,
the new line begins a little way in from the ones immediately
above. Each of these lines starts a new paragraph.

A PARAGRAPH SHOULD CONTAIN A NUMBER OF SEN-
TENCES ALL CONNECTED IN THE SENSE THAT THEY ARE
RELATED TO ONE TOPIC OR THEME.

Say where new paragraphs should begin in the following:

The police decided to set a trap for the shop-lifters at my father's shop in Fore Street. This meant that Angela had to be there to identify the suspicious characters she had seen last week. After tea a plain clothes detective took up his position and began to do some stock-taking. Angela was told to sweep up, and my father was in his usual position behind the counter. During the next half-hour several people came in and bought sweets and tobacco. No one tried to steal anything, and Angela gave no sign that she recognised anyone. It must have seemed a waste of time to my father. Suddenly the whole situation changed. Two women came in with large carrier-bags and leant across the counter. When one of them asked for a box of chocolates, Angela dropped her broom. This was the signal that she recognised the women. My father turned his back to the shelves to fetch the chocolates and one of the women stretched out her hand towards a pile of cigarettes. But she didn't pick them up, she suddenly drew back her hand and shouted at Angela, 'Why stare at me in that suspicious way?' Both of them left the shop. The detective felt these were probably the guilty women but he hadn't been able to catch them red-handed.

6. Looking at Paragraphs

When you first think of ideas for story-writing or composition work, they spring to mind in any order, all jumbled together. But before you write down these ideas they must be put in the right order. They must be planned so that the reader can follow your ideas. They must be arranged in paragraphs according to an obvious and orderly plan.

(a) Re-arrange the sentences below according to an obvious and orderly plan. Do not alter the sentences themselves.

My room on the second floor is just what I wanted.

My father met us on the door step.

We went upstairs.

We had a meal as soon as we arrived.

Mother turned out the light and I went to sleep.

I read a chapter of my book in bed that night.

(b) Charlie Hunter chose *My holiday* as a subject for a composition. He noted down his ideas for paragraphs without thinking out an orderly plan. Re-arrange his paragraph plan giving the correct order of events.

MY HOLIDAY

Leaving home on Saturday.

First glimpse of France from the air.

The scene at London Airport.

French porters.

Taxi ride through Paris to our hotel.

The customs.

Ordering an evening meal at our hotel in Paris.

A day's sightseeing in Paris on Sunday.

To the South of France by coach.

The scene at London Airport

(c) Give paragraph plans for two of the following subjects:

    Mending a puncture   Sports day

    A narrow escape   A visit to a hospital

    Scotland Yard   My own room

(d) Write the three opening paragraphs on the two subjects in Exercise 6 (c) which you chose for your own paragraph plan. Remember that each paragraph should contain a number of sentences all connected in the sense that they are related to one topic or theme.

(e) Write the final paragraph for the *ending* of any one of the subjects in Exercise 6 (c) above.

7. Alphabetical Order

Arrange these words in strict alphabetical order:

    knob comb calm   island   listen   should

    tunic way   chancel compass apparently solo

Write each of them in a sentence and make sure you can spell all of them correctly.

8. Things to Do and Research Work

Give the name of any book or film which features a detective as one of the main characters.

Find out who wrote the music for *On Wings of Song*.

Write out correctly five words which you spelt wrongly in Exercise 6 (d) above.

Name any two films or T.V. plays which have been based on a book.

Name an author alive today who writes books for adults.

Prepare notes for a four-minute lecture on *Keeping pets*.

Find the composer of the music for *On Wings of Song* in your WHO'S WHO.

Say who lives in these places: 10 Downing Street, London The Vatican   Buckingham Palace   The White House

7

An Unwanted Customer

IT ALL STARTED because Angela saw a small wicker basket
in the corner. On Fridays after school we usually go down
to Fore Street to help tidy up the shop. I was in the stockroom at the back and Angela was sweeping up.

When she had opened the basket she went over to ask
my father what to do with it.

'I can't imagine who left that behind,' he said. 'Just see
what's inside, Angela, and then give it to John to put in the
stockroom. Somebody will call back for it tomorrow.'

Angela went back to examine the open basket. 'It's quite
empty,' she said.

At that moment a man rushed into the shop.

'Put that basket down!' he shouted.

'All right, sir, nothing to worry about,' remarked my
father.

'Put that basket down,' repeated the man, more quietly.
'I happen to know that it contains an adder, the only
poisonous snake in England!'

I stood still in the stockroom doorway. There was a sudden tense silence in the shop. Then my father went into
action. No questions; no panic; only commands.

'Stand still where you are, Angela and John! You, sir,
guard the door into the street and grab yourself a walking-
stick from that rack! Your snake is *not* in that basket. It
must be somewhere in this room.'

Then he walked quietly over to us and took the broom from Angela's hands. They were trembling a bit and so were mine. For three tense minutes four pairs of eyes searched the floor of the shop and my father went carefully over every inch of it.

Suddenly I felt Angela shudder beside me. She gripped my arm and swallowed hard. I expected a scream, but instead a small voice said,

'I can see your snake—up there, look, by the cage.'

And there it was, slithering slowly over the shelf towards the budgerigars.

Again my father went into action. 'Well done, Angela! Stay still, both of you. Now, sir, can you capture him alive, or shall I finish him off with this broom?'

'Leave him to me,' came the answer. Then the stranger moved quietly across from the door and went behind the counter. Slowly he raised his arms. Both the budgerigars and the snake seemed too interested in each other to notice him. The next moment he had the snake in his hands. One hand behind its head, the other round its tail. Then he put it back in the basket.

'Quite an expert bit of snake-catching, sir,' said my father. I must say I felt very proud of my father and of Angela, they both had been so sensible and brave.

It turned out that this man was from the country zoo a few miles away. He had come to Summervale to collect the adder from some gipsies who had found it on the common. Naturally he knew how to handle snakes, but it was pretty careless of him to leave the basket in our shop. It was only for a few minutes, but even so it might have been very serious!

Anyhow he was a most friendly person and invited

Angela and me to visit him at the zoo during the holidays.

After all this excitement I only just remembered to ask my father about the shop-lifters. Apparently they were caught red-handed in Wilson's draper's shop in Fore Street. What a pity it did not happen in *our* shop!

I don't suppose I will write much in my diary for quite a time now. We have to revise for the end of term tests!

1. Reading for Meaning

When the news of the unwanted customer in the Freemans' shop was reported in the SUMMERVALE NEWS, the B.B.C. T.V. news team came down to interview the family. These are the questions the Freemans were asked. Give the answers.

(a) Now, tell me, Mr Freeman, who first discovered the basket?

(b) What did your father say, John, when a stranger rushed shouting into the shop?

(c) What weapons did the two men have in their hands?

(d) What did you do and say, Angela, when you first saw the snake?

(e) How did our friend from the zoo grasp the snake?

(f) What did your father say when the snake was safely back in its basket?

(g) Who told you that the snake was a poisonous adder?

(h) Do you think you children will ever see the snake again?

(i) One last question, John. What makes you say you are proud of your father and your sister Angela?

2. Detective Reading and Discussion

(a) When did the snake escape from the basket?

(b) How did Mr Freeman know that the snake was not in the basket?

(c) How do you know that the stranger was an expert snake-holder?

(d) Is there any cure for an adder's bite?

(e) Can you give one fact about the skin of a snake and one about the tongue of a snake?

(f) What is the name of non-poisonous snakes found in Great Britain?

(g) Why is there an exclamation mark (!) after the word *down* in line 13?

(h) Suggest another title for this chapter.

(i) Explain the meaning of *shudder sensible careless*.

3. Reading for Pleasure

Read the following verses from D. H. Lawrence's poem, *Snake*.

A snake came to my water-trough
On a hot, hot day, and I in pyjamas for the heat,
To drink there.

He reached down from a fissure in the earth-wall in the gloom
And trailed his yellow-brown slackness soft-bellied down,
over the edge of the stone trough
And rested his throat upon the stone bottom,
And where the water had dripped from the tap, in a small
clearness,
He sipped with his straight mouth,
Softly drank through his straight gums, into his slack long
body,
Silently.

FOR DISCUSSION

(a) Which words in this poem do you think are particularly well-chosen and especially descriptive of a snake?

(b) Try to discover the meaning of the word *fissure* without looking it up in a dictionary.

(c) This verse of D. H. Lawrence's poem has no rhymes. Compare the poems in Chapter 2 and Chapter 6 (p. 16 and p. 41).

4. Looking at Paragraphs

In Chapter 6 (p. 43) you were told that *a paragraph should con-*

D

tain a number of sentences all connected in the sense that they are related to one topic or theme.

With this in mind, write one paragraph of between five and ten sentences on any three of the following:

Angela Freeman　　Budgerigars　　Summervale
A snake　　An old village street　　Washing-day

5. Tricky Words

Write each of the following words in a separate sentence:

either　　neither　　receive　　height　　feign

6. Dictionary Work

Look up each of these words in your LITTLE DICTIONARY at the back of this book and write each in a separate sentence:

trough　　fissure　　predicate　　apparatus　　hero

Story Writing

(a) Write an exciting story in which you or someone in your family is the main character or hero. Give it a title.

(b) Describe in four paragraphs how the police caught the two shop-lifters red-handed in Wilson's draper's shop in Fore Street, Summervale.

8. Things to Do

Say what apparatus you need for each of the following:
Underwater swimming　　Washing-day　　Bird-watching
Name three daily newspapers and say what each costs.
Look up D. H. Lawrence in your WHO'S WHO.
Make up a short poem about an animal or a bird.
Find out some facts about Mr Ionides and the book *Snake Man* by Alan Wykes.
Read the passage about the Black Serpent in the book *Far Away and Long Ago* by W. H. Hudson.

8

The End of Term

THIS DIARY OF MINE—*John Freeman's Diary*—will never be like the one Samuel Pepys wrote. I just don't have time, and now the end of term tests are here. So I shall have to be content to record a few dry facts about our family and leave it at that. Here they are.

I did get word to our choirmaster, Mr Hunter, about Angela. She was allowed to take the singing test but she came second. So she won't be singing the solo in *On Wings of Song* at the schools' choir festival in Summervale Church as we all had hoped.

The Freeman family photograph appeared in the SUMMERVALE NEWS with a whole column on our snake fight in the shop, and the B.B.C. showed their interview with us on the T.V. news.

And now for the end of term and the Christmas holidays!

*

A NOTE BY THE AUTHORS

You can check your answers to the questions in Exercises 1 and 2 on the next page by using the page reference given in brackets at the end of each question. Charlie Hunter got eight answers right. See if you can do better than he did.

Now turn over and begin your test!

*

1. (a) How far is Summervale from Buckingham Palace? (p. 9).
  (b) How do you know that Mr Freeman has been in the Royal Navy? (p. 10).
  (c) Name the street where Mr Freeman has a shop (p. 25).
  (d) Who is choirmaster at Summervale Church? (p. 34).
  (e) How old is Angela Freeman? (p. 19).
  (f) What is an adder? (p. 46).

2. (a) Mention three facts about a sentence (p. 12).
  (b) Who wrote *David Copperfield*? (p. 13).
  (c) When must you use a full stop? (p. 18).
  (d) Give the subject of this sentence: The lion roars (p. 22).
  (e) Who wrote *Alice in Wonderland*? (p. 24).
  (f) Name the punctuation mark at the end of each of these remarks: Who are you? How strange! (p. 30).
  (g) How can you tell when a new paragraph begins? (p. 42).
  (h) Name 4 kinds of sentences (p. 37).

3. Write each of the words printed in Exercise 3 on page 21 in a separate sentence.

4. Make sure you can spell all the Tricky Words in Exercise 5 on page 50.

5. Write five sentences about each of the following:
    Guy Fawkes Day   Christmas   A busy street
    An empty house   The moon   Food

6. Write one paragraph of not more than ten sentences on each of the following:
    Opening my Christmas presents.   Washing-up.
    Trying on a new coat in a shop.   How to mend a puncture.
    Watching the television or listening to the radio.

7. Write two paragraphs on each of the following:
   (a) *Two views of Summervale.* From outside Mr Freeman's shop and from the roof of the Freemans' new home.
   (b) *Before and After.* What Angela and John Freeman thought their new schools would be like and how they really turned out to be.
   (c) *The Beginning and the End.* Starting out from home for a day's outing and returning home in the evening.

8. Write three short paragraphs on (a) and (b) below:
   (a) John Freeman, Angela Freeman, Charlie Hunter.
   (b) Myself aged four years; myself today; myself in ten years' time.

9. Name the title of the chapter you enjoyed most in this book so far. Give reasons for your choice.

10. Read Chapter 6, *A Visit from the Police*, again. Now write down what Angela might have written in her diary about all this. (Remember she is ten years old.)

11. I was completely lost in a dense fog when I met my friend from next door. I recognised him by the white stick he always carried. How was it my friend guided me home so easily?

12. Use each of these words in a separate sentence to show the meaning clearly:
   gondola   weary   precious   tunic   mingle   delicate

13. Find out why 13 is supposed to be an unlucky number.

14. Who wrote: *Little Women, The Pied Piper of Hamelin, Pepy's Diary, On Wings of Song?*

15. Write a story on one of the following:
   A storm at sea   London in 1998
   Bicycle thieves   A narrow escape

9

A Visit to the Zoo

I MUST in honesty record in my diary that the famous Freeman family and the snake affair were soon forgotten. Newspaper photographs and T.V. interviews are concerned with other families now. The Freemans are no longer news!

The end of term tests went quite well for me, and the very first weekend of the holidays Angela and I went to the country zoo. We saw 'our' snake, of course, and much more besides. We are not just ordinary visitors! Mr Peters, the man who left that adder in our shop, took us behind the scenes.

As a result of this, I've given up the idea of helping in my father's shop when I leave school. I want to be a vet. instead. I decided this today, after talking to the animal keepers at the zoo.

Angela left me and went to ride elephants and to watch the seals, while I stayed with the keepers and went with them on their rounds. Of course, I wasn't allowed in any of the cages, but I saw something of the keepers' work.

They had a sick monkey called Beppo. Apparently these delightful creatures catch cold very easily and poor Beppo was seriously ill. I was allowed to take him in my arms and I am sure he smiled and felt better when I held him. The keeper was pleased and asked me to persuade Beppo to take his medicine. This was successful too, so perhaps I could be trained to make a good vet.? But what about dogs and cats, not to mention horses and cows?

No doubt in a year or so I shall change my mind again and go back to the idea of helping in my father's shop when I leave school.

We had a magnificent tea and we both met the 'zoo-quest' man, David Somebody. Angela says he is by far the best grown-up in the world apart from our family. He took us seriously, talked *normally* and was genuinely interested in us. So unlike the many grown-ups who seem to 'talk down' to people of my age! There was no pretending or nonsense about him.

I like the head of the zoo, Mr Peters, very much, and there was some talk of visiting the children's hospital to entertain the patients with some of the zoo pets. I wonder if I can be one of the helpers for this occasion. I must ask my mother the best way to find out if Mr Peters wants help from 'John Freeman, a strong, hard-working, honest, clean and animal-loving lad, aged 14 years'!

1. Reading for Meaning
(a) Where did John and Angela Freeman go on the first week-end of their holidays?
(b) What did Angela do besides watch the seals?
(c) What was the name of the sick monkey?
(d) Why does John use the word *apparently* in the sentence, *Apparently these delightful creatures catch cold very easily*?
(e) What is meant by *talking down*?
(f) What is the full word shortened here to *vet.*?
(g) Give this passage another title.

2. Detective Reading and Discussion
(a) Why is it that the Freeman family are no longer news?

(b) How do you know that John has not decided what work to do when he leaves school?

(c) Do you think John is fair in his remark that *many grown-ups seem to 'talk down' to people of my age*?

(d) Can you suggest how John can find out if Mr Peters wants help when he takes some pets to the children's hospital?

(e) If you were writing the last sentence in the passage for your own diary, how would you describe yourself?

(f) Would you rather be a vet. or a shop-keeper? Give reasons.

3. Reading for Pleasure

Read these five lines from a poem by Tennyson:

> Willows whiten, aspens quiver,
> Little breezes dusk and shiver
> Thro' the wave that runs for ever
> By the island in the river
> Flowing down to Camelot.

FOR DISCUSSION

Can you feel and hear a definite rhythm?

Read these lines from *Hiawatha*, a long poem by Longfellow.

> Swift of foot was Hiawatha;
> He could shoot an arrow from him
> And run forward with such fleetness
> That the arrow fell behind him!

FOR DISCUSSION

Can you hear and feel the rhythm in these lines of poetry? Why do you think there is an exclamation mark (!) at the end?

4. Looking at Sentences

(a) From the last paragraph in the passage in this chapter, *A Visit to the Zoo*, pick out one sentence which is a statement, one which is a question and one which is an exclamation.

(b) Look at these sentences:
   (i) He has two sons. He has one daughter.
   (ii) He has two sons *and* one daughter.

NOTICE: When making a single sentence by using the joining word *and* there is no need to repeat *He has*.

5. Looking at Paragraphs

Write single paragraphs on each of the following topics. Include two or three single sentences which have a number of different joining words.

Riding an elephant	A hospital
A thunderstorm	Trying on a new dress

6. Tricky Words: Got

Find a better word for *got* in each of the following sentences:

Charlie got a prize.	We got a goal.
Angela got there late.	I got an ice-cream at the shop.
John has got a diary.	I got a cold yesterday.

7. Things to Do

Prepare a three-minute talk on one of the topics in Exercise 5 in this chapter.

Find out how wild elephants are captured. Consult a book by Gladys Davidson called *Catching Wild Animals Alive*.

Look up Tennyson in your WHO'S WHO.

Mention three rules you need when crossing a road.

Explain why doctors insist that everyone should always wash their hands before a meal.

Find Longfellow's poem *Hiawatha* in a poetry book and read some more verses.

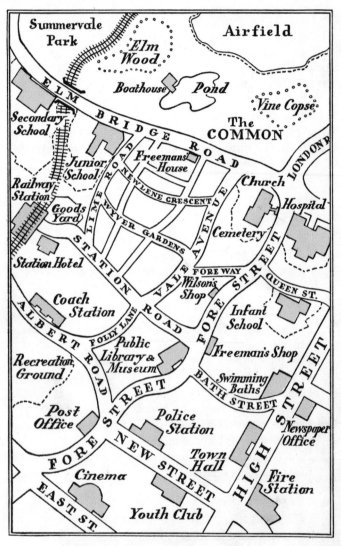

John Freeman's map of Summervale

58

10

The Map of Summervale

INSTEAD OF WRITING anything in his diary this week, John Freeman drew the map of Summervale which is printed on the opposite page.

1. Study this map of Summervale and then give accurate and clear instructions for reaching the stated places from the first place mentioned.

From the Town Hall to the hospital.

From the Town Hall to the Secondary School.

From the Coach Station to the Freemans' house.

From the Coach Station to Mr Freeman's shop.

From the Freemans' house to the Swimming Baths.

From the Freemans' house to the Primary School.

From the Freemans' house to the hospital.

2. (a) Describe the view from the west windows of the ward on the top floor of the hospital.

(b) Name the buildings and shops in Fore Street which runs from south to north (London road).

(c) What improvements would you suggest that might help the flow of traffic coming from the south towards London?

(d) What other buildings would you like to see put up in Summervale?

(e) Describe or draw the position of your school in relation to your town or village.

3. Reading for Pleasure

Even when a mere child I began my travels, and made many tours of discovery into foreign parts and unknown regions of my native city. As I grew into boyhood I extended the range of my observations. My holiday afternoons were spent in many rambles about the surrounding country. I visited the neighbouring villages, and added greatly to my stock of knowledge by noting their habits and customs. I even journeyed one summer's day to the summit of the most distant hill where I stretched my eyes over many a mile of unknown country.

Washington Irving

FOR DISCUSSION

(a) Examine the following five sentences:

   I made many tours of discovery.

   As I grew into boyhood I extended the range of my observations.

   My holiday afternoons were spent in many rambles about the surrounding country.

   I even journeyed to the summit of the most distant hill.

   I stretched my eyes over many a mile of country.

   Notice the importance of the words *tours*, *extended*, *rambles*, *summit*, *stretched* in helping you to make these sentences vivid, interesting and colourful. Can you find any other words in the passage which do this?

(b) Try reading Washington Irving's first sentence aloud with expression and rhythm.

(c) Describe what the passage is about in three sentences.

(d) In the first sentence the author uses the word *travel*. He also uses other words which suggest travelling. Can you find three words which do this?

(e)   What is meant by?
        My native city   Habits and customs
        I extended the range of my observations
        Added greatly to my stock of knowledge

4. Understanding English: Capital Letters

Notice the use of capital letters in the following four pairs of sentences:

(a)   There is a new boy in our class.
        The new boy is called Charlie Hunter.
(b)   There are seven days in a week.
        Is Monday the first day of the week?
(c)   There are twelve months in the year.
        The last month is December.
(d)   There are many monkeys in the zoo.
        My favourite monkey is called Beppo.

Now make up eight sentences using one of the following pairs in each: e.g. We find the most beautiful *country* scenes in *Scotland*.

country	Scotland	river	Thames
county	Yorkshire	girl	Angela
town	London	Beppo	monkey
mountain	Everest	ocean	Pacific

Notice that when words belong to a special place or person they always begin with a capital letter, whatever their position in the sentence.

Which word in *every* sentence must *always* begin with a capital letter?

5. Tricky Words: Abbreviations

When you write formal sentences and paragraphs do not use shortened forms of words (abbreviations).

But in writing notes and diaries and in addressing envelopes these shortened forms are useful. You will come across them in other books. Give the meaning of the following abbreviations:

£. s. d.	T.V.	S.O.S.	Col.	Notts.
M.P.	B.B.C.	&	B.C.	U.S.A.
V.C.	etc.	cwt.	vet.	e.g.

Notice the use of full stops with abbreviations.

6. Dictionary Work

(a) Look up the meaning of the following words in your LITTLE DICTIONARY at the back of this book:

tour   observe   ramble   vivid   crisis
native   rhyme   rhythm   narrative   anxiety

Write each of them in a separate sentence.

(b) Arrange the following words in strict alphabetical order:

college   castle   cabin   call   calf   camp   calm

7. Things to Do

(a) Look up Washington Irving in your WHO'S WHO at the back of this book.

(b) Look at Exercise 6 in Chapter 6. Now give six headings (to make six topics in a paragraph plan) for:

Exploring my native city (or village).

(c) Write the first three paragraphs, based on your own topic headings above, on *Exploring my native city (or village).* Try to make your sentences in these paragraphs vivid, interesting and colourful. Read the *Improve Your Speech* section below before you begin.

8. Improve Your Speech

Read this sentence aloud, learn it by heart and practise speaking it clearly and with meaning.

A sentence is a group of words expressing a complete thought, while a paragraph contains a number of sentences all connected in the sense that they are related to one topic or theme.

11

Emergency Ward

JUST AFTER MY father came in from work at seven o'clock last Tuesday evening, my mother suddenly collapsed on the floor. I have never been so frightened in my life, and Angela began to cry, which made things worse.

My father went into action quickly and calmly. He told Angela sternly to stop crying and fetch a glass of water. He told me to help him to lift Mother into a chair. Then he telephoned Doctor Janson.

In five minutes the doctor arrived. My mother was deathly pale, but able to put her hand on her right side and whisper, 'A terrible pain just here, doctor'. He wasted no further time. He rang up the hospital for an ambulance and arranged for her to be admitted to the emergency ward at once. I heard my mother ask, 'Does it mean an operation?' And I saw the doctor nod in reply.

About an hour later my father returned from the hospital. 'They're operating now, it's a burst appendix,' he announced. He sounded quite calm and matter of fact, but Angela and I knew how upset he really was. His left eye was twitching, always a sign of nerves with father.

Poor Angela found it difficult to stop crying and I was shaking like a leaf and biting my nails.

'Now you two, lend a hand. I will make some stew and rice pudding. I'll ring the hospital later. Something to do will help us to stop worrying,' we were told. We were also

kept busy thanking neighbours for their offers of help. They had seen the ambulance and were all most kind. Rather different from that time when they saw the police car outside our home!

Late that night my father rang the hospital. From my bed where I lay awake I heard him ask, 'And just what do you mean by *as comfortable as may be expected*? Obviously he was not satisfied with the official answer to his questions. Finally he came up and told me, 'Your mother's doing fine'—but I saw that he was still terribly worried and upset.

Indeed, we had three days of real anxiety before the doctor called in to tell us that Mother was out of danger and would be home in another ten days. How relieved we all were! No more twitching eyes, nail biting and crying!

By this time we had all come to realise how much depends on a mother for the smooth running of a home. However, we managed fairly well and kept things going between us. Father was cook, Angela shopped and made the beds, and I washed up and hoovered the rooms.

1. Reading for Meaning

(a) If it takes Mr Freeman fifteen minutes to walk home from his shop, at what time did he leave the shop last Tuesday evening?

(b) Why did Mr Freeman speak *sternly* to Angela?

(c) How did Mr Freeman show his true feelings of anxiety?

(d) How many telephone calls were made from the Freemans' home last Tuesday evening? Who made them?

(e) What expression does John use to show that he himself was desperately worried and upset?

(f) Why do you think Mr Freeman told John, *Your mother's doing fine*?

(g) What does Mr Freeman consider to be a good way to help people to stop worrying?

(h) John says they *kept things going* in the home. Does this mean that everything was 100 per cent. efficient? Discuss this expression.

(i) John uses the words—*upset*, *worried* and *anxious* to describe their feelings. What words does he use about his father's voice and his father's actions at this time of crisis?

2. Detective Reading and Discussion

(a) How was Mrs Freeman taken to hospital?

(b) How do you know that Mr Freeman went to the hospital with his wife?

(c) On which side of the body is the appendix?

(d) Explain what John means by the neighbours' behaviour last Tuesday being *rather different from that time when they saw the police car outside our home*? (Refer to Chapter 6, p. 39, if you cannot remember.)

(e) Why did John know his father was not satisfied with the *official hand-out*?

(f) John says of his father, *I saw that he was still terribly worried and upset.* What did John actually *see*?

(g) How do you know from this chapter that Mr Freeman was well-trained to deal with an emergency?

(h) Discuss what day-to-day organisation is required to make the smooth running of a home.

(i) Mention some of the things you do to help in the day-to-day running of your home.

(j) Mention some of the ways in which pupils can help in the day-to-day running of a school.

3. Letter Writing

Read this letter which John Freeman wrote to Mr Peters at the country zoo. *John forgot to put in the date.* Write today's date in your exercise book and punctuate it correctly.

> 3 Elm Bridge Road,
> Summervale,
> S.W.24.

Dear Mr Peters,

Angela and I very much enjoyed our visit to your zoo. It was very kind of you to let us go behind the scenes, and I hope Beppo the monkey is better now.

You did mention taking some of the pets to the hospital to entertain the children there. I remembered this because my mother has just been taken to hospital for an operation. Do you think that Angela and I might be allowed to help you?

I hope you don't mind my asking directly like this, and I will quite understand if you think we are too young and inexperienced.

> Yours sincerely,
>
> John Freeman

Below is the answer which Mr Peters sent to John Freeman. *Mr Peters has left out something in the date.* Add what is needed together with any necessary punctuation.

Downside Country Zoo,
Belmont,
Near Summervale.
19th February.

Dear John,

Thank you for your letter. I am so glad you and Angela enjoyed your visit to our zoo. Do come again! The keepers and the animals all took pleasure in meeting you both and would like to see you next time you visit us.

I had hoped to take Beppo and some of the other animals and birds to the hospital to cheer up the children there. But I now learn that this cannot be allowed. The danger of infection from germs which the animals might carry is too great. So my grand idea has come to nothing.

Certainly we would have taken you and Angela to help us. It was sensible and correct of you to ask me directly. After all, if people don't make a few polite requests like this they will never get anywhere!

With best wishes to your family and I do hope your mother will soon be well enough to return home.

Yours sincerely,

J. F. G. Peters

FOR DISCUSSION

(a) Notice the position of the address, and that a separate line is used for the beginning, *Dear Mr Peters*, and for the ending, *Yours sincerely*, and for the signature, *John Freeman*. Notice also the use of commas and capital letters in the address at the top right-hand corner, and after the beginning and ending.

(b) Beginnings and endings of letters vary. The words used for
relatives and close friends will be different from those used
in more formal letters like those above. Business letters will
be even more formal.

  Discuss the following beginnings and endings: Dear Sir;
My dearest Cousin Tom; Darling Angela; My dear Charlie;
Yours very sincerely; With love from; Yours faithfully;
Yours ever; Yours affectionately.

4. Addressing Envelopes

Rule three areas of $5\frac{1}{2}$ in. by $3\frac{1}{2}$ in. Now fill in the addresses in
these spaces for (i) Mr Peters; (ii) Mrs Freeman (in Summervale
Hospital); (iii) Mr Wilson (the draper in Fore Street).

  Discuss the various ways of addressing envelopes—the position of each line, the commas, etc.

5. Understanding English: Common and Proper Nouns

Examine these three sentences:

  The new boy is called Charlie Hunter.

  The last month is December.

  My favourite monkey is called Beppo.

They are printed in Exercise 4 in Chapter 10, p. 61, to show
that words belonging to a *particular* person, animal, place or
thing all begin with a capital letter. Now consider the list below:

NAME	PARTICULAR NAME
boy	Charlie
man	Mr Peters
mountain	Everest
city	Edinburgh
girl	Angela
monkey	Beppo
river	Thames

In fact, all the naming words in both these columns are
called NOUNS when they are used in sentences for naming any
person, animal, place or thing.

In the left-hand column, the names are all COMMON NOUNS: names of places, people, animals or things.

In the right-hand column, the names are all PROPER NOUNS: names of *particular* places, people, animals or things.

EACH PROPER NOUN MUST BEGIN WITH A CAPITAL LETTER

(a) Copy the following list and fill in the common nouns in the left-hand column, using the proper nouns on the right as clues.

COMMON NOUNS	PROPER NOUNS
	Mrs Freeman
	Scotland
	Atlantic
	Monday
	December
	Comet
	Paris

(b) Write down:

Three common nouns that name things you like to eat. Put each in a sentence and underline it.

Three proper nouns that name three of your friends.

Three common nouns that name things in the classroom. Put each in a sentence and underline it.

One proper noun that names each of the following:
a country, a lake, a river, a girl, a boy, a man, a month, a cricketer, a swimmer, an animal.

(c) Punctuate the passage below, putting in all the necessary capital letters, full stops and commas:

on monday mrs freeman returned from summervale hospital she had a suitcase a carrier bag and a bunch of flowers mr hunter kindly drove her home past our shop in fore street and she said she felt like queen elizabeth setting out from buckingham palace for a holiday in scotland she made a cup of tea on arrival

6. Tricky Words

Write each of the following words in a separate sentence:

sincerely	affectionate	cousin	signature
received	friend	address	envelope
vivid	paragraph	sentence	February

Underline these words in your sentences and make sure you can spell them.

7. Story Writing

(a) Make the outline below into a full-length story using vivid sentences and at least three paragraphs. Give your story a title. (Refer to the picture on the page opposite.)

Outside Mr Freeman's shop. Cat on wall by pavement in sunshine. Dog on opposite side of road. Car coming down street. Dog sees cat. Dog rushes across road in front of car. Cat sees dog. Driver of car sees dog. Cat rushes into Mr Freeman's shop. Budgerigars see cat. Mr Freeman sees dog. Dog chased out of front door. Cat taken to back door. Budgerigars settle down. Empty street outside.

In your story you may use proper nouns instead of the common nouns, dog, cat, driver, if you wish.

(b) *Either* make up a story featuring a police car chasing a robber's car and a narrow escape at a level-crossing, *or* write an exciting story called *Adventure in a Fog*.

8. Things to Do

(a) Find an anthology of poems. Look through the *Contents List* and write down the names of any poems you have met before. Turn to one of them and read it.

(b) Write down two suitable subjects for a poem.

(c) What is the difference between a newspaper and a magazine?

(d) Prepare notes for a four-minute lecture on any subject you like or know something about.

Street scene outside Mr Freeman's shop

12

Back to Normal

MY MOTHER HAS been home from hospital for a week now.
She is much stronger but we have to try to stop her doing
too much work in the house. She is anxious to get things
back to normal as soon as possible.

Angela has taken charge of the shopping and my father
does the cooking. I shall be glad when he gives up this job
as we seem to live on a succession of stews and rice pudding. This means that I have a particularly heavy wash-up,
which is my job in the house at the moment. I think we all
realise now who is the most important person in our house!

At school we have a tape-recorder in our classroom and
we are going to do a radio play and record it for a broadcast to other forms in the school. I haven't a speaking part
but hope to take a lead with Charlie Hunter in the 'Effects
Department'.

Since the radio play we are recording has been broadcast, I wrote to the B.B.C. for advice about the music and
noises off-stage, and received a most helpful reply.

Now I am preparing my short talk to the rest of the class
on *Playmaking for the Radio*. Charlie suggested that I write
down my talk and then learn it by heart, only using notes
while I am actually speaking.

This seems a good plan, and my notes will be based on
the following draft which I have written down with the
help of the reply sent to me by the B.B.C.

Ladies and Gentlemen,

You can learn a great deal about producing plays for the radio by listening to those which are actually broadcast, and by making experiments in your classroom here. We cannot make a perfect broadcasting studio; but by using screens to divide the audience from the players we will be able to give an effective and enjoyable performance.

The most important thing to remember is that our play must be brought to life through *sound* only—by the voice *and* by the use of sound effects.

The 'Effects Department' needs careful planning. Sounds can create the background of the story, such as the noise of waves breaking on the sea-shore, the whirr of machinery, the rustling of trees, heavy footsteps, horses' hooves, the smashing of crockery, and so on.

To add to the effect, recorded music can be used at the opening and closing of the play and to show a pause in time during the action of the play.

I suggest we form a small group to organise the 'Effects Department' and rehearse carefully with the speakers (actors). As you all know, we have chosen a dramatic incident from *The Silver Skates* by Mary Dodge for our performance next month.

1. Reading for Meaning

(a) Why do you think Mrs Freeman needs to be stopped from doing too much in the house?

(b) Why does John object to stew and rice pudding?

(c) Who has been acting as cook, as shopper, as dishwasher while Mrs Freeman was in hospital?

(d) Who is the most important person in the Freeman house?

(e) What is meant by *an effective performance*?

(f) How can a radio play be *brought to life*?

(g) How can an 'Effects Department' help a Radio Play?

2. Detective Reading and Discussion

(a) Discuss the work Mrs Freeman usually does in her house. How much, and in what ways should the rest of the family continue to help when everything is back to normal?

(b) Is it more difficult to act in a radio play or a T.V. play?

(c) What sort of recorded music would you use at the beginning and ending of each of these radio plays and features:

A Smash and Grab Raid	Listen with Mother
Spring comes to Summervale	Life on the Farm
A Christmas Nativity Play	Hospital Casualty Ward
The Battle of Trafalgar	Jo and the Skiffle Group

(d) Is it best to use notes and learn a talk by heart or read what you have prepared from a written statement? Give reasons.

(e) What is the value of a chairman at a public meeting?

(f) Consider the detailed work of the Effects Department for two of the Radio Plays mentioned in (c) above.

3. Reading for Pleasure

Read this poem, *Laughing Song*, by William Blake:

When the green woods laugh with the voice of joy,
And the dimpling stream runs laughing by;
When the air does laugh with our merry wit,
And the green hill laughs with the noise of it;

When the meadows laugh with lively green,
And the grasshopper laughs in the merry scene,
When Mary and Susan and Emily
With their sweet round mouths sing, 'Ha, Ha, He!'

When painted birds laugh in the shade,
Where our table with cherries and nuts is spread,
Come live, and be merry, and join with me,
To sing the sweet chorus of 'Ha, Ha, He!'

FOR DISCUSSION

(a) Compare the rhythm of Blake's poem with the lines by Tennyson and Longfellow on page 56.

(b) Do you think Spring is a more joyful time of year than Autumn?

(c) Why is the poem *The Highwayman* called a narrative poem? (Refer to Chapter 6.) Is Blake's *Laughing Song* a narrative poem?

4. Understanding English: The Subject Word

(a) Write down the subject in each of these sentences:
     The lion roars.   The wheel turns.

(b) Notice the subjects underlined in the following sentences: What is the rest of the sentence called?

   The red book is a dictionary.

   The old tree was struck by lightning.

   The drowning man clutched an oar.

(c) Which is the one most important word in each of the subjects underlined in (b) above? (It is a naming word, i.e. a noun.)

(d) Write down the subject in each of the sentences below. Then underline the one most important word in each. In these sentences it will be a naming word, a common noun or a proper noun, but this is not always so.

   My young sister is called Angela.

   Poor Mrs Freeman went to hospital.

   The beautiful, yellow dress was a great success.

   The tall, powerful swimmer won the race.

NOTICE THAT THE MOST IMPORTANT WORD IN THE SUBJECT OF EACH SENTENCE IS CALLED THE SUBJECT WORD.

(e) Study the subject words underlined in these sentences. Which two subject words are *not* nouns?

My best <u>friend</u> won a prize.

<u>Angela</u> has a beautiful voice.

Near the door stood <u>Charlie</u>.

<u>We</u> went to London.

<u>You</u> must win the race.

(f) Which subject words in Exercise (e) above are common nouns and which are proper nouns?

(g) Place one of these subject words in each of the sentences below: *river   they   Hans   skates   friend*

At school my best . . . . . . is Charles Hunter.

The winding, rushing . . . . . . made a waterfall.

. . . . cheered when Angela won the prize.

Little . . . . came from a poor family in Holland.

The flashing, silver . . . . . . sped over the ice.

5. Tricky Words

(a) Examine these words and write each in a sentence to show you understand the meaning.

     don't   I'll   can't   it's   he's
     I've   she's   aren't   I'd   we'll

Notice that an apostrophe is placed where a letter (or letters) is missed out.

Finish this list using each of the words above:

     don't   is used for   do not
     I'll   is used for   I shall (or I will)

(b) Notice that we say: *a* lion   *an* owl   *a* mouse   *an* elephant

Say whether we use *a* or *an* with each of the following:

     fish   eagle   Englishman   plate   umbrella   cousin
     inch   turnip   apron   uncle

In fact we generally use *an* before a word beginning with one of these letters: a, e, i, o, u (which are called vowels).

(c) Write each of these words in a sentence so that the meaning
     of each is clear: its   their   your

6. Improve Your Speech!

Read over John Freeman's talk in Chapter 12, BACK TO
NORMAL, beginning *Ladies and Gentlemen*. Then try reading
it aloud.

You will find the information in this talk useful for Chapter
13, which is the actual Radio Play *The Silver Skates*, as broadcast by the B.B.C., to which John Freeman refers.

7. Dictionary Work

Look up these words in your LITTLE DICTIONARY at the
back of this book and write each of them in a separate
sentence: chairman   vowel   experiment   advice

8. Things to Do

(a) Write a letter, with your own address in the top right-hand
     corner at the beginning, from Angela or John Freeman to
     mother in hospital, telling her how the work in the Free-
     man house has been organised in her absence.

(b) Write a letter from John Freeman to the B.B.C. asking for
     advice about the Effects Department for a Radio Play. Use
     your own address.

(c) Address the envelope for the letters in Exercise 8 (a) and
     (b) above.

(d) Look up William Blake and Mary Dodge in your WHO's
     WHO.

(e) Find out how to make a rice pudding.

The Silver Skates

THE SILVER SKATES

MARY DODGE

★

CAST

THE NARRATOR

KATRINKA

PETER
HILDA } (aged 14–15 years)

CARL

DAME BRINKER (middle-aged)

DR BOEKMAN (middle-aged)

CRIER

HANS BRINKER (aged 15)

GRETEL BRINKER (aged 12)

CROWD OF CHILDREN

★

13

The Silver Skates

NARRATOR: What would come into your mind at once if someone said, 'Windmills—canals, dykes—tulips?' 'Holland', I expect! Now, if you're interested in that country you must read *Hans Brinker or The Silver Skates*. The book gets its name partly from the 15-year-old Dutch boy who is the hero, and partly from the Silver Skates, coveted prize in a skating match for young people, on the frozen River Y (*pronounced 'Eye'*), a few miles from Amsterdam.

On the cold December morning when the story opens a merry group of girls and boys came racing along the canal on their way to school. Their bright costumes made them look like a gay tulip bed, while their gleaming skates flashed in the bright keen air. Suddenly they stopped as they saw another of their friends.

VARIOUS VOICES (*excited*): Katrinka! Oh, Katrinka! Have you heard of it? The race—we want you to join!

KATRINKA: Race? What race?

[*Excited gabble of voices from which emerge words 'Hilda', 'Silver Skates'*]

KATRINKA: Oh, please, don't talk all at once. I can't understand. What do they mean, Peter?

PETER: Why, we're to have a grand skating match on the 20th. Hilda has arranged it all, and ...

ANOTHER VOICE: It's for her mother's birthday!

ANOTHER VOICE: Yes, and Mevrouw (*Meffrow*) von Gleck is going to give a splendid prize to the best skater . . .

TWO OR THREE VOICES: Beautiful—beautiful silver skates—with silver bells and buckles.

SMALL BOY'S VOICE: *Who* said they had bells?

VOICES: They have.

OTHER VOICES: They haven't.

KATRINKA (*laughing and exasperated*): What are they *really* like, Hilda?

HILDA: The pair for girls *will* have silver bells.

VOICES: See—I told you.

HILDA: But there's to be another pair for the boys—without bells, but with an arrow engraved on the sides.

VOICES (*rather overcome by such magnificence*): Oh! *Two* pairs of silver skates.

KATRINKA: And who's to compete in this race?

PETER: All of us. You must try too, Katrinka.

KATRINKA (*laughing*): We'll see! Now, who can beat me today on the last half-mile to school?

[*Laughter becoming less in the distance*]

HILDA: Why don't you go with the others, Carl?

CARL: Oh, there's no hurry—you and I can follow and still be in good time. (*Mockingly*) I say, look at this pretty pair coming along the ice. They look like rag-pickers. Did you ever see such skates?

HILDA (*gently and reprovingly*): Poor things—it must be very hard to skate on such queer affairs. I expect the boy made them himself.

CARL (*mumbling and somewhat ashamed*): I shouldn't wonder.

HILDA: The girl's a pretty little thing.

CARL: Humph!

HILDA: I'm going over to speak to her. Coming?

CARL (*sulkily*): Not I! I'm off.

HILDA: Little girl! What's your name?

GRETEL (*somewhat overawed*): Gretel, my lady. And this is my brother, Hans.

HILDA (*brightly*): Hans looks as warm as a stove, but you seem to be cold. You should wear more clothing.

GRETEL (*shivering but bravely*): I'm not so little—I'm past twelve.

HILDA: I'm nearly fourteen. (*Concerned*) But you're shivering.

HANS: My sister has not complained, but (*sadly*) this is bitter weather.

HILDA: I really stopped you to ask if you'd like to enter for the grand race.

HANS: What race, young lady?

HILDA: It's for my mother's birthday. I'm Hilda von Gleck. We're giving two pairs of silver skates as prizes. Now, won't you enter? You both skate so well.

HANS: If we did try we'd skate only a few strokes. You see, our skates are hard wood. They soon become damp.

GRETEL: And then they stick and trip us.

HILDA (*generously and warmly*): I do wish I could buy each of you a really good pair of skates but I'm afraid I've been very extravagant with my allowance this month.

HANS and GRETEL: Oh, thank you—but we don't want ...

HILDA (*clink of money*): Still there's enough left to buy *one* pair. Take this, Hans, and get the skates for the one who is most likely to win the race. Good-bye!

F

HANS (*calling*): Jufvrow! (*Yuffrow*) Jufvrow von Gleck! You are very good, but we cannot take this money.

HILDA (*calling*): Why not indeed?

HANS (*proudly*): Because we have not earned it.

HILDA (*quickly*): You want to earn it? Then carve me a wooden chain like the one Gretel wears round her neck.

HANS (*eagerly*): I will, Jufvrow, and you shall have it to-morrow.

HILDA: Now I must hurry or I'll be late for school. Good-bye Hans and Gretel.

GRETEL (*clapping her hands in delight*): What a good young lady! You must go to Amsterdam tomorrow and buy the skates—for yourself.

HANS: No—I mean *you* to have them. Then you will practise hard—and my little Gretel shall win the silver skates.

GRETEL (*laughing delightedly*): Oh, Hans!

NARRATOR: When Gretel got her new skates, and a lovely warm red jacket from Hilda there wasn't a happier girl in Holland. Then Peter decided that *his* little sister needed a carved chain like Hilda's, so two days later Hans had enough money to buy himself skates—but he hesitated.

They were so very poor—his father had been a help-less invalid for years—his mother worked like a slave, spinning and knitting. He himself worked on the land, and Gretel tended geese for the neighbouring farmers. Even so, they only just managed to live. No wonder then, that Hans looked at the money, and argued with his mother.

HANS: I cannot buy skates, Mother, while you need so many things—feathers, and wool, and meal, and . . .

DAME BRINKER: That will do, Hans. Your silver cannot

buy everything. But (*sighing*) if only our stolen money could be found.

HANS: You really think it was *stolen*, Mother?

DAME BRINKER: Aye—for if your father hid it about here I must have found it long ago.

GRETEL: True, Mother.

DAME BRINKER: I sometimes wonder if your father paid it away for the great silver watch we have guarded ever since the day of his accident—but surely not. The watch isn't worth a quarter of our money.

HANS (*muttering*): Where *did* that watch come from?

DAME BRINKER (*sadly*): That we shall never know, for I have shown it to your Father many times, but he does not know it from a potato—just stares and smiles.

GRETEL: Tell us again about the first time you saw it.

DAME BRINKER: I have told you so often—it was that dreadful night of the storm ten years ago. Father came in drenched and tired, and pulled out the watch from his coat. 'Here good wife,' said he, 'take care of this until I ask for it again,' and then ... (*sobbing*)

GRETEL (*softly*): Yes, Mother?

DAME BRINKER: Before he could say any more Broom Klatterboost came rushing in here with: 'Haste, Raff Brinker. The floods are up. The dyke is in danger.'

HANS: And of course he went.

DAME BRINKER: Aye—he snatched up his tools and ran. And that was the last time I saw him in his right mind. He was brought in near midnight—he had fallen from the high scaffolding on the dyke.

GRETEL: Oh, poor Father!

DAME BRINKER: His head was all bruised and cut. In time the wounds healed, but his mind and memory were gone.

HANS: All these years you have worked and struggled—and never sold that watch.

DAME BRINKER: No—for dear Father might wake and ask for it.

HANS: Wake, Mother? Wake and know us?

DAME BRINKER (*softly*): Aye, child, such things have been known.

HANS: Then we must never give up the watch, (*more cheerfully*) and perhaps the lost money may come to light when we least expect it.

GRETEL: Was it *much* money, Mother?

DAME BRINKER: It was everything we had scraped and saved—one thousand guilders.

HANS and GRETEL: A thousand guilders!!

DAME BRINKER: We kept it in an old stocking in the big chest there. And after your father was hurt and I needed the money so badly, I found the chest—empty (*tragically*).

HANS (*comforting*): Don't worry, Mother. Gretel and I will soon be able to work so hard that we'll have all we need; and we'd rather see you bright and happy than have all the silver in the world.

GRETEL: Yes, indeed Hans.

DAME BRINKER: Now off with you for your skates, Hans. What keeps you now?

HANS: I was thinking that this money might bring a doctor from Amsterdam to see Father—and perhaps cure him.

DAME BRINKER: A doctor would not come for thrice that money. Now go, Hans.

NARRATOR: So Hans set off for Amsterdam on the old

wooden skates, and, as luck would have it, he met, skating towards him, a very famous man, whom he recognized from the pictures in shop windows—Dr Boekman, the greatest physician and surgeon in Holland. He looked grim and stern, but something urged Hans to speak to him.

HANS: Dr Boekman.

DR BOEKMAN (*grimly*): Yes?

HANS: Sir, I know you are a famous doctor. I have to ask a great favour ...

DR BOEKMAN: Hm! Get out of the way. I've no money, and never give to beggars.

HANS (*proudly*): I am no beggar, sir, and I have money, see. (*Clinking his silver in his hand*) I wish to consult with you about my father.

DR BOEKMAN: Your father, eh? Is he ill?

HANS: His body is well, sir, but his mind is sick. He is a living man, but sits like one dead.

DR BOEKMAN (*kindly*): Hey? What? Tell me then, boy.

HANS: It was in the great floods, ten years ago ...

[*Fade out voices—then bring up again*]

HANS: Oh, do see him, sir. I know this money is not enough, but take it, sir. I will earn more—I will toil for you all my life if you will cure my father.

DR BOEKMAN (*gently*): Put away your money, boy. I will see your father.

HANS (*sobbing with joy*): Oh, thank you, sir.

DR BOEKMAN: Where do you live?

HANS (*eagerly*): A mile south of Broek, sir, near the canal. And thank you, sir—a thousand blessings on your kindness.

DR BOEKMAN: Good-bye, boy. Do not expect too much,

good-bye. (*To himself*) Hopeless, I fear, but young Hans pleases me—reminds me of my poor little boy Laurens. (*Sighing*) I cannot forget that scamp in spite of his folly, and his ingratitude. The boy looks just as *he* did at that age ... [*Pause*]

Music

HANS (*excited*): Mother! Gretel! Great news for you!

GRETEL: You've got your skates, Hans? Show me!

HANS: Far more important. On my way to Amsterdam I met Dr Boekman on the ice—and, Mother—I stopped him and told him about Father.

DAME BRINKER (*horrified*): The great Dr Boekman. You never dared to speak to *him*?

GRETEL (*incredulous*): Hans!!

HANS: I did, and what's more he's coming to see Father, and he'll cure him if he can be cured.

DAME BRINKER: I won't believe it till I see him here.

GRETEL: He looks very stern in his pictures. Was he angry when you spoke to him?

HANS: At first; but he grew quite kind and gentle.

DAME BRINKER: I believe that the great man has had his troubles too. Someone told me that he lost his only son —but that's a long time ago. No—I don't think he died. He disappeared, and after that Dr Boekman changed— became cold and hard. But if he cures Father I shall pray for him and bless him every day.

GRETEL: And so shall I.

HANS: Do you think that Gretel and I could go out and practise together with our new skates?

GRETEL: It isn't long now to the 20th you know, and the race for the silver skates.

DAME BRINKER: Well—just for an hour. Then you must come in to bed.

HANS: Come Gretel—I'll race you.

[*Sound of running feet*]

DAME BRINKER (*to herself*): They're good children. But if only my poor Raff could know us again!

NARRATOR: Did Raff Brinker ever recover his senses? Did the family ever find the lost guilders? Who was the owner of the mysterious watch which they had preserved for ten years? Did Dr Boekman ever hear any more about his son? You will find all the answers when you read the book—and very exciting and surprising they are.

But, you say—especially if you are a skater—what about the other bit of the story—The Silver Skates? Well, the account of the race is fascinating, and there's only time to give you the briefest glimpse of it.

CRIER (*reading rules in a loud voice*): The girls and boys will race in turn until one girl and one boy has beaten twice. They start in a line from the united columns— skate to the flagstaff line, turn, and come back to the starting point, thus making a mile at each turn.

PETER: Stand here, Hans, and we'll see Mevrow von Gleck drop her handkerchief—then the bugler will give the signal.

HANS: There goes the handkerchief, Peter.

[*One blast of bugle*]

PETER and HANS: They're off!

*[Silence for a moment, then music again,
then cheering growing louder]*

HANS: Gretel! Gretel!
PETER: Hilda! Gretel!

[Great roar of cheering]

CRIER: Gretel Brinker, one mile.
VOICES: Gretel Brinker! Gretel Brinker! Gretel has won the Silver Skates!
HANS: Oh, Gretel, I'm so proud of you, little sister.
GRETEL: Oh, Hans, it's like a fairy tale come true. Now if only you could win the other prize . . .

NARRATOR: Don't you wonder if he did? Well, you know how to find out!

14

Swimming Sports

CHARLIE HUNTER AND I were chosen to act as stewards at the Summervale Junior Schools swimming sports yesterday. They were held at the new Public Swimming Pool which had just been built in Summervale. Before the sports, Sir Richard Benson, a famous actor, opened the new baths officially.

When I first heard this, I thought it was rather silly to ask an actor, but our local Director of Education introduced Sir Richard as a great swimmer who had once represented Britain in the Olympic Games! It just shows how careful one has to be before jumping to conclusions!

Sir Richard told us of some of his experiences in international competitions, and of his stage performances in Shakespeare, too. He gave a wonderful speech. As he talked he seemed quite carried away by his descriptions of nerve-racking occasions on the stage and in the water. Gradually he moved nearer and nearer to the edge of the pool behind him. Finally, at a dramatic moment in his speech, Sir Richard took a step backward! He fell, best suit and all, into the clear water below!

There was a dreadful silence followed by a few giggles before he surfaced. Then, as his head bobbed up, he shouted, 'I declare this pool well and truly opened!' He was grinning all over his face. Everyone roared with delight, realising at once he had fallen in on purpose. It was a wonderful bit of acting.

'I declare this pool well and truly opened'

After this dramatic opening came some exhibition high diving. This was equally spectacular and breath-taking. How I wish I could dive properly! Perhaps now we have this wonderful pool in Summervale I shall learn more quickly. But I'll never dare to do a somersault from the top board!

My job as steward was to call the names of the competitors over the speaker system and ask each group to line up at the start. In the last race but one, the name of my sister, Angela Freeman, was on my list for the back-stroke.

Angela is a good swimmer, but she was in the under-twelve-years group, and as she is only ten, some of the other girls were bigger and stronger. However, she did very well, and managed to come third. I saw my mother and father sitting at the far end and looking very proud of their daughter who won a medal.

As a matter of fact, they were proud of me, too! They told me that my speech was much improved and that I had a good radio voice. Perhaps I shall apply for a speaking part in our next radio play at school, although I prefer to be in charge of the Effects Department.

Mother has taken over running the home again now, but my father and I still take turns in helping with the washing-up in the evenings. It's a boring job, but it is the least we can do to help a bit in the house. I've already suggested a washing-up machine on the H.P., but Father won't buy anything he can't pay for in full at the time.

1. Reading for Meaning

(a) Was Sir Richard Benson a good choice for the official opener of the new baths? Give reasons.

(b) What exactly does John mean by being careful before *jumping to conclusions*?

(c) How can you tell from John's description that Sir Richard was a good actor?

(d) *He was grinning all over his face.* Consider why this sentence is more effective than: He was smiling broadly, or He was grinning.

(e) What instrument did John use to call the competitors to the start of each race?

(f) Why were Mr and Mrs Freeman proud of Angela and John?

(g) What does the abbreviation H.P. stand for?

(h) Suggest another title for this chapter.

2. Detective Reading and Discussion

(a) What sort of nerve-racking experiences might Sir Richard Benson have had during his stage career?

(b) How do you know that Sir Richard was a Shakespearean actor?

(c) Discuss Angela's feelings as she waited at the start of the back-stroke race.

(d) Why does John think he might apply for a speaking part in the next radio play at school?

(e) Discuss the advantages and disadvantages of buying expensive labour-saving machines for the home on H.P. terms.

3. Reading for Pleasure

Read these lines taken from Robert Browning's poem, *The Pied Piper of Hamelin*.

> Small feet were pattering, wooden shoes clattering,
> Little hands clapping and little tongues chattering,
> And like fowls in a barnyard when barley is scattering,
> Out came the children running.
> And all the little boys and girls,
> With rosy cheeks and flaxen curls
> And sparkling eyes and teeth like pearls,
> Tripping and skipping ran merrily after
> The wonderful music with shouting and laughter.

FOR DISCUSSION

(a) Which words describe the appearance of the boys and girls?

(b) What words are used to show that the children were hurrying, and to show they were happy and excited?

(c) Do you think this is a narrative poem?

(d) What happened *before* the children followed the Pied Piper?

(e) What is meant by *flaxen curls*?

4. Understanding English: Verbs

(a) In Chapter 11 you examined the work of those words which name people, animals, places or things in sentences. What are these words called?

(b) Read through Exercise 5 in Chapter 11.

(c) Now examine the work of the words underlined in the following sentences:

The lion <u>roars</u>.   The wheel <u>turns</u>.

The man <u>clutched</u> the oar.   Charlie <u>won</u> the race.

NOTICE:

These underlined words (called *verbs*) work as *telling* or *doing* words. They tell us about ACTION.

(d) Look at the verbs underlined in these sentences:

Charlie <u>was</u> chairman.

Winston Churchill <u>became</u> Prime Minister.

Angela <u>felt</u> nervous.

John <u>seemed</u> worried.

The aeroplane <u>was</u> high.

England <u>is</u> a country.

They <u>made</u> him chairman.

These underlined words (verbs) help to express *condition*. They tell what the person, animal, place or thing named by the subject *is* or *was* or *became* or *felt* or *seemed*.

WORDS WHICH WORK AS DOING WORDS, TELLING US ABOUT ACTION OR CONDITION, ARE CALLED VERBS.

In fact, every sentence we write is about somebody or something doing something or being something.

(e) Examine the verbs in the following sentences and say how they differ from the verbs in Exercises (c) and (d) above.

Angela <u>was singing</u> a solo.   What <u>are</u> you <u>laughing</u> at?

I <u>have put</u> my suit away.   Hans Brinker <u>is winning</u>.

NOTICE: Verbs sometimes consist of more than one word.

(f) Make two columns headed SUBJECT and PREDICATE. Then split each of the following sentences into subject and predicate and write each part in the correct column.

The girls shopped in the market.

Edinburgh is in Scotland.

Near the door stood Charlie.

The beautiful old tree fell down.

Why are you crying?

(g) Underline the verbs in your predicate column in (f) above.

(h) Write down the one subject word in each sentence in (f) above.

(i) Pair the following nouns and verbs to make five sentences, adding any other words (*the*, *a*) that are necessary:

NOUNS   lion, sun, cows, postman, dog.

VERBS   is shining, are grazing, roars, barked, knocked.

5. Looking at Sentences

Remember that there are four kinds of sentences:

statement   question   command   exclamation

Say which of the following are sentences and which are not and give reasons. (Full stops have been left out to make it more difficult.)

With great speed   Hurry up!
Who won the prize?   A rolling stone
The boys went swimming   Beyond the gate
Near the door stood Angela The lion roars

6. Punctuation

Punctuate the following putting in the capital letters, commas, full stops and exclamation marks where necessary.

the swimming gala was held at the summervale public baths this year and angela freeman won a prize and so did charlie hunter when the chairman announced the winners of the sprint free-style back-stroke and diving there was great applause how john cheered after it was all over they went home tired and happy and mrs freeman prepared an excellent supper for john and angela

7. Story Writing

Choose one of the three following endings and use it in a short story. Make the ending you choose the last sentence.

'I shall never forget you,' said the stout old gentleman, 'for you saved my life.'

'The mistake you made,' said the detective, 'was to leave your boots under the bed.'

So Mary was chosen to take the lead in the Hollywood film.

8. Tricky Words: Nice

Use a better word than *nice* in each of the following.

We had a nice holiday.   The weather was very nice.

We had nice meals and nice rooms.   We saw a nice picture.

We arrived back in nice time for dinner.

It was a nice journey.

9. Things to Do and Research Work

(a) Look up Robert Browning in your WHO'S WHO.

(b) Look up the meaning of these words in your LITTLE DICTIONARY and write each word in a separate sentence:
flaxen   barley   reign   disqualify

(c) Find out who is the Prime Minister of Great Britain at the moment.

(d) Draw a picture of the scene described in the poem, *The Pied Piper of Hamelin*, in this chapter.

(e) Look at the first sentence of this chapter *Swimming Sports*. Now read through the punctuation Exercise 6 which contains a deliberate mistake of fact. Can you spot it?

(f) Prepare notes for a four-minute talk on *Life-Saving*.

(g) Look up in a poetry anthology the poem William Blake wrote called *Tiger*, and read it.

(h) Explain: a fly-over, a roundabout, a subway, a viaduct, a motorway, a service road, a by-pass, a junction, a road 'filter', a cul-de-sac.

(i) Draw diagrams to show as many road signs as you know and name each in block capitals.

(j) There is a series of Radio Plays in seven books called *May We Recommend* which may be in your school, and you may be able to read some of these, or perhaps to 'perform' them.

15

Fire

THERE WAS A FIRE in Summervale last Thursday, and we were all very excited about it in different ways. The fire was at Wilson's Draper's shop in Fore Street. My father is friendly with Mr Wilson, so he was very upset about the fire. On the other hand, I could not help enjoying the sight, which was quite spectacular. Fortunately, there was no-body in the building when it caught fire. This is the account of the blaze given in our local paper, which I have pasted into my diary.

A fire broke out last night in the premises of Messrs. Wilson and Sons, the drapers in Fore Street. The alarm was given by a passer-by who noticed smoke pouring out of the windows of a showroom on the first floor. It was thought at first that the fire was a minor out-break, but it soon appeared that it was very serious, having started at the back of the shop. By the time the alarm was given and answered, the flames had taken a thorough hold of the building.

A large crowd gathered, amongst them Mr Wilson, the owner, who was compelled to watch the destruction of premises which had been in the hands of his family since 1873.

In spite of the efforts of the Fire Brigade, it was not long before the flames attacked the front of the shop, and the firemen were obliged to give their attention to

The fire in Fore Street

saving the adjoining buildings. Huge clouds of thick smoke rose into the air above the burning shop, and rolled away, obscuring the stars. Amidst the smoke, enormous tongues of orange-coloured flame shot upward and outward, roaring like a fierce animal devouring its prey. Now and again there was a crash, followed by tremendous showers of golden sparks as a beam collapsed inside the doomed building.

In the thick atmosphere the shadowy forms of the firemen could be seen as they directed powerful jets of water to the flames. After three hours they managed to bring the fire under control. It proved impossible to save anything from inside the shop, and after a long struggle between men and their ancient enemy, all that was left of Mr Wilson's property was a water-logged ruin, black and useless. Fortunately for the owners, the property was fully insured.

Interviewed by our reporter, Mr Wilson said that the firm would rebuild on the same site, and in the meantime they would be carrying on business in the empty premises at 149 Fore Street, formerly the Aston Cinema.

1. Reading for Meaning

(a) Where, and at what time of day, did the fire break out?
(b) How was the fire first noticed?
(c) Where did the fire begin?
(d) What is the meaning of *a minor outbreak* of fire?
(e) To what does the writer compare the tongues of orange-coloured flame?
(f) Why was it fortunate for the owners that the property was fully insured?
(g) What does *obscuring the stars* mean?

(h) The report calls the burnt-out shop *a water-logged ruin, black and useless*. Complete these sentences:

> The building was water-logged because ...
> The ruins were black because ...
> The shop was useless because ...

(i) Where did Mr Wilson intend his new shop to stand?

(j) How do you know from the newspaper account that all Mr Wilson's stock was destroyed by the fire?

(k) Suggest a suitable headline for the newspaper report.

2. Detective Reading and Discussion

(a) Suggest three possible causes of the fire at the shop.

(b) Did Mr Wilson live in a flat over his shop or in a house some distance away? Give reasons.

(c) Explain the old saying, *Fire is a good servant but a bad master*.

(d) How old, *at least*, was the burning building?

(e) The report compares fire to *a fierce animal devouring its prey*. Can you think of other things with which you can compare fire?

(f) Give a list of the words in the report which mean *very large*.

(g) The reporter calls the shop *the doomed building*. How does this show that the report was written *after* all was over?

(h) Describe exactly what you would do if you were the first to notice a building on fire.

(i) Was an ambulance called to the scene of the fire? Give reasons for your answer.

(j) Describe what policemen do in order to:

control traffic	patrol their beats
divert traffic	guard empty premises
arrest criminals	see children across the road
control a crowd	answer enquiries
assist the firemen	direct strangers

(k) How would the firemen protect the adjoining buildings?

3. Reading for Pleasure

Here are four verses from the long poem, *The Ancient Mariner*,
by Samuel Taylor Coleridge.

> Down dropt the breeze, the sails dropt down,
> 'Twas sad as sad could be;
> And we did speak only to break
> The silence of the sea!
>
> All in a hot and copper sky,
> The bloody sun, at noon,
> Right up above the mast did stand,
> No bigger than the moon.
>
> Day after day, day after day,
> We stuck, nor breath nor motion;
> As idle as a painted ship
> Upon a painted ocean.
>
> Water, water, everywhere,
> And all the boards did shrink;
> Water, water, everywhere,
> Nor any drop to drink.

FOR DISCUSSION

(a) Have you read the story of the *Ancient Mariner*? Can one
of you re-tell it?

(b) What words help to make a particularly vivid picture of the
sun?

(c) To what is the idle ship compared?

(d) Why could they not drink the water which was every-
where?

(e) Why did the boards shrink?

(f) Discuss the rhythm in the verses.

(g) What are the rhyming words in each verse and in which
lines do they always come?

4. Looking at Words

Give six words or associations which spring to mind for each of the following: traffic speed ambulance flames thirst

5. Understanding English: The Predicate Word

(a) First check carefully your understanding of:

Subject and Predicate	(Chapter 3, Exercise 5, p. 22)
Subject Word	(Chapter 12, Exercise 4, p. 75)
Nouns	(Chapter 11, Exercise 5, p. 68)
Verbs	(Chapter 14, Exercise 4, p. 92)

(b) Now look at the two sentences below:

The young girl shopped in the market.

The old oak tree fell to the ground.

From each of these sentences pick out: the subject, the predicate, a noun, the subject word, a verb.

IN EACH SENTENCE THE MOST IMPORTANT WORD IN THE PREDICATE—*The Predicate Word*—IS THE VERB

(c) Because the verb is the most important word in the predicate, the choice of the right verb in sentences helps your writing to be vivid and clear.

e.g.   The snake *glides* along.

I *toured* the neighbourhood.

I *stretched* my eyes over many a mile.

Give suitable predicate words—VERBS—for each of the following sentences, e.g. My best friend *won* a prize:

The pony . . . across the fields.

The cat . . . under the chair.

The river . . . its banks after a storm.

The doves . . . in the trees.

The swimmer . . . to the shore exhausted.

The waves . . . on the shingle.

6. Tricky Words

Write each of the following 12 words in a separate sentence to show you understand its meaning:

rain	reign	their	there
were	where	sent	scent
chord	cord	here	hear

7. Alphabetical Order

Arrange all the words in Exercise 6 in strict alphabetical order.

8. Reading and Writing

(a) Write a newspaper report, complete with headlines, based on *either* the drama of the snake in Mr Freeman's shop (refer to Chapter 7), *or* on Mrs Freeman's sudden illness (refer to Chapter 11).

(b) Write an advertisement for the local newspaper offering a second-hand bicycle for sale.

(c) Write a greetings telegram to Mrs Freeman's mother in Camberwell on the occasion of her 80th birthday.

(d) Look up Samuel Taylor Coleridge in your WHO'S WHO.

(e) Write a story describing how you rescued a small child from drowning at the seaside.

(f) Make up a few verses of a poem on any subject you like, and give it the same rhythm and the same arrangement of rhymes as *The Ancient Mariner*.

(g) Copy out and complete the puzzle below by answering the clues given beside each.

As idle as a —— ship

| P | | | | E | |

A 'doing' word is one

| | | | B |

A 'naming' word is one

| | O | |

Charlie's surname

| | | | | E | |

He kept a diary in 1665

| | | Y | |

16

Nothing to Report

THERE WAS A LONG gap in *John Freeman's Diary* after the fire you read about in the last chapter. He was training for athletics three evenings a week and spent a lot of time at the Summervale Youth Club. Angela told us that he also went to Charlie Hunter's home quite frequently, especially at weekends, and she added that Charlie Hunter's sister was very pretty. Not a word of all this is to be found in John's diary—the only entry for four weeks was NOTHING TO REPORT—and then he suddenly started writing again (see Chapter 17). What happened during those four weeks remains a mystery.

1. Finding out facts about the Freemans

(*Refer to the page reference given in brackets after each question only if necessary or to check your answers.*)

(a) Where did the Freemans live before moving? (*page 9*)

(b) What is Mr Freeman's occupation? (*page 14*)

(c) How old is John? (*page 20*)

(d) How old is Angela? (*page 19*)

(e) What is the name of John's school friend? (*page 20*)

(f) What did Mr Freeman do before setting up in business? (*page 10*)

(g) What housework did John and Angela do when Mrs Freeman was in hospital? (*page 65*)

(h) What part did John take in the Radio Play, *The Silver Skates*, at his school? (*page 72*)

(i) What is Angela good at besides singing? (*page 90*)

2. Prove it!

Refer to the Chapter given in brackets after each statement below and then quote the evidence from the chapter to prove that what is printed below is true.

(a) John was good at handling monkeys. (*Chapter* 9, p. 54.)

(b) John and Angela always knew when their father was upset. (*Chapter* 11, p. 63.)

(c) Mr Freeman can cook, but not as well as his wife. (*Chapter* 12, p. 72.)

(d) John Freeman saw Sir Richard Benson in a wonderful bit of acting. (*Chapter* 14, p. 89.)

(e) Angela is a promising swimmer. (*Chapter* 14, p. 90.)

(f) Mr Wilson the draper was not ruined by the fire at his shop. (*Chapter* 15, p. 98.)

(g) John is keen to do well in athletics. (*Chapter* 16, p. 103.)

(h) John wrote nothing in his diary for four weeks. (*Chapter* 16, p. 103.)

3. Understanding English

(*Check your answers by the references given in brackets.*)

(a) Name four kinds of sentences. (*Chapter* 5, *Exercise* 5, p. 37.)

(b) Give three examples of an abbreviation. (*Chapter* 10, *Exercise* 5, p. 62.)

(c) Give examples of: a common noun and a proper noun. (*Chapter* 11, *Exercise* 5, p. 68.)

(d) Give the subject word and the predicate word in this sentence: My best friend won a prize. (*Chapter* 12, *Exercise* 4 (e), p. 76, and *Chapter* 15, *Exercise* 5 (c), p. 101.)

(e) Give the abbreviations for: do not I will cannot it is he is I have she is are not (*Chapter* 12, *Exercise* 5, p. 76.)

(f) Say whether we use *a* or *an* in front of each of the following: owl mouse elephant lion (*Chapter* 12, *Exercise* 5 (b), p. 76.)

(g) Give the verb in this sentence: Angela felt nervous. (*Chapter* 14, *Exercise* 4 (d), p. 93.)

4. Letter Writing

(a) Explain with an example how to write your address correctly at the top of your notepaper.

(b) Explain with an example how John Freeman should address the envelope for a letter to his history master.

(c) Write a letter and address the envelope to a friend in the local hospital.

5. Reading for Pleasure

(a) Choose one of the poems printed in any of the Chapters 1 to 15 and learn four or five lines by heart.

(b) Make up four or five lines of poetry or prose on any subject you like and then write down some points arising from your poem or prose under the heading FOR DISCUSSION.

(c) Make up two or three titles for adventure stories likely to appeal to eight-year-olds.

(d) Give a list of three famous authors of (i) books, (ii) poems, (iii) plays. You need *nine* authors in all.

(e) What newspaper would you recommend your twin brother to read?

6. Sentences and Paragraphs

(a) Give an example of a complete sentence and say what it must contain.

(b) Explain the use of paragraphs in writing a story or composition.

(c) Write four sentences about each of the following. (Be vivid, colourful and accurate.)

The setting of the sun seen at the seaside.

Spring and the first cuckoo.

An express train going through a tunnel.

A frail, sick monkey.

A kindly old woman selling flowers outside Woolworths.

(d) Write two paragraphs about one of the subjects in (c).

7. Story Writing

(a) Write a story on one of the following subjects and give it another title.

A Cowboy A Horse A Nurse A Dreadful Flood Swimming the Channel Meeting the Queen A Ghost

(b) Finish this story and give it a title:

Just about midnight a policeman on his beat in Fore Street, Summervale, thought he saw a flash of light in a jeweller's shop. He quickly tried the door and . . .

(c) Write the story of your life between the ages of twenty and thirty.

(d) Write a short account of what you think John Freeman was doing during the four weeks he wrote nothing in his diary.

8. Things to Do and Research Work

(a) Find out how John Freeman ought to carry out his training for athletics.

(b) Describe accurately the everyday clothes which either John *or* Angela might wear on a seaside holiday.

(c) How is 13 written in Roman numerals?

(d) Name various styles of haircuts for either boys or girls. Point out the advantages and disadvantages.

(e) Find out the cost of each of the following:

1 lb of tea   1 lb of butter   1 lb of rice

a pair of nylon socks or stockings

a journey by rail (2nd class) from your nearest railway station to Edinburgh

driving over 30 m.p.h. in a built-up area

a dog licence   a toothbrush   one orange

a copy of Shakespeare's *Twelfth Night* published by Penguin Books.

(f) Find out the meaning of the word *charity* as it is used in the Bible, *I Corinthians XIII*. Read this passage, or find someone to read it aloud to you.

17

Angela goes to Town

MY SISTER ANGELA still does the family shopping on Saturdays, and yesterday she had an extraordinary adventure on her way home.

She had finished the shopping and was looking for Old Strummer. He is a little old man who plays an ancient piano which he pushes round the streets of Summervale on a handcart. Angela told me that when she spotted Old Strummer and was just about to rush after him, she dropped her fully-laden shopping basket. Everything rolled out on the pavement. Quickly she gathered up the parcels, but to her horror she saw a large, brown dog making off with the Sunday joint.

Angela left her basket on the pavement and gave chase. Eventually she rescued the meat. It was a bit the worse for wear but at least it was safe. By the time she reached her basket again she saw two grinning boys strolling across the road munching loudly. They had stolen our biscuits and cake while Angela had been recovering the Sunday joint. Not only that, but they had just placed her shopping basket in the middle of the road, right in the line of the traffic.

By the time Angela had everything under control again, the boys had disappeared. Angela said she recognised one of them and was determined to deal with him later.

By this time Old Strummer had parked himself outside Woolworths and had started to hammer away on the yellow keys. Angela joined him, and he was delighted to see her again. Yesterday she decided to sing while Old Strummer played. She carefully hid the Freeman shopping basket under some sacking on Old Strummer's handcart before she began to sing.

Old Strummer and Angela

Neither Angela nor Old Strummer realised that there was a film unit across the road taking shots of Summervale and recording a programme about *New Towns in Britain*. It was the usual rather dull street-corner interview stuff followed by the playing of a record chosen by a local inhabitant.

However, while all this was going on three things happened almost at once. Angela started to sing while Old Strummer played; the film producer saw and heard them across the road; and Angela caught sight of the boys who had stolen the biscuits and cake.

But I will have to write up the rest of this amazing adventure in my diary some other time. First I must check all the details from Angela and Old Strummer so that I can record an accurate account of these startling events in my diary about the Freeman family.

1. Reading for Meaning

(a) What does John mean when he writes that Angela saw a dog *making off with the Sunday joint*?

(b) In what ways do you think that the parcel of meat was *a bit the worse for wear*?

(c) What did Angela have to do to get everything under control?

(d) Why did Angela hide her shopping basket under the sacking?

(e) What is meant by *local inhabitant*?

(f) Explain what is meant by *taking shots of Summervale*.

(g) As soon as Angela started singing she saw the boys who had stolen the biscuits and cake. What words does John use instead of the verb *saw* in this sentence?

(h) Suggest another title for this chapter.

2. Detective Reading and Discussion

(a) How much do you think the Freeman Sunday joint cost?

(b) Why does Old Strummer *hammer* the keys of his ancient piano?

(c) Do you agree with John that the sort of street interviews he mentions are *rather dull*?

(d) Why did John break off his diary so suddenly?

(e) Do you know any police regulations about singing or selling in the streets?

(f) What do you expect the film-unit producer to do now that he has seen and heard Old Strummer and Angela?

3. Reading for Pleasure

Read these lines written by Aldous Huxley

Moonless, this June night is all the more alive with stars. Its darkness is perfumed with faint gusts from the blossoming lime trees, with the smell of wetted earth and the greenness of the vines.

FOR DISCUSSION

This is written as prose, not poetry. Yet the choice of words and the order of words gives it a poetic flavour. The form in which it is written has a natural beauty and it is a true description. But it is more than a mere description; it makes us feel and imagine this quiet June night. Can *you* feel and understand this?

4. Understanding English: Singular and Plural Nouns

(a) What is the difference between the nouns underlined in these two sentences?

Angela lost her basket.   Angela lost her baskets.

(b) Notice how the nouns below which refer to one thing change when they refer to more than one thing.

boat	boats	inch	inches
house	houses	fox	foxes
table	tables	shop	shops

WHEN A NOUN REFERS TO ONE THING IT IS SAID TO BE *in the singular*.

WHEN A NOUN REFERS TO MORE THAN ONE THING IT IS SAID TO BE *in the plural*.

(c) Give the plural of these singular nouns:

field   cow   dog   bat   hedge   book

(d) Give the singular of these plural nouns:

boxes   matches   fishes   glasses   potatoes

(e) Look at Exercises (a) and (b) above and discuss why some nouns form a plural by adding *es*, others by adding *s*.

5. Tricky Words

Write each of the following words in a separate sentence:

ought   caught   brought   thought   daughter

Underline these words in your sentences and learn to spell them.

6. Dictionary Work

Look up the following words in your LITTLE DICTIONARY at the back of this book. Write each in a sentence.

ancient	dwarf	onlooker	tint	programme
ranch	steer	envious	russet	obstinate

7. Writing and Reporting

(a) Write down the *answers* to these questions put to Summervale's oldest inhabitant by a member of the film unit recording the programme on *New Towns*.

Tell me, Mr Robinson, how old are you?

Have you lived in Summervale all your life?

Tell us about the day the first motor car drove through Fore Street.

What were your feelings when they built the new airfield?

What do you think of the modern houses put up on the new estate at Summervale?

What are your views about the young people of today?

(b) You suspect that men from the next ranch have been branding your cattle with their own marks. One day you and one of your men surprise three men in a hollow about to brand a young steer. Describe what happens.

(c) Report on the costume you have chosen to wear at a Fancy Dress Party for the local newspaper.

(d) Write a story called *The night we left the tap running*.

(e) Explain exactly how one of the following works:

a camera   a bicycle pump   a fountain pen   a torch

(f) Choose one of the following and explain how to:

light a fire   sew on a button   make a pot of tea

(g) Give a report to the police on a street accident you have just witnessed.

8. Additional Work for those who have time

(a) Choose a further subject from Exercise 7 (e).

(b) Choose a further subject from Exercise 7 (f).

18

Angela's Triumph

ANGELA KNEW THAT if she stopped singing and chased the two boys who had stolen our biscuits and cake they would escape easily enough into the crowd. What she did *not* know was that her performance with Old Strummer on his piano was being filmed all this time. Her eyes were on those two boys.

She moved back to the handcart and picked up Old Strummer's cap. She knew exactly what she was going to do now. Slowly she moved forward among the crowd, still singing as she collected money in the cap. At last she stood within reach of the enemy. Suddenly she stopped singing pounced forward and gripped each boy tightly by the hair, dropping the cap as she did so. At the same time she shouted with all her might, 'These two pinched my parcels and can jolly well pay me back!'

The crowd thought it all a huge joke, all part of the act, and began to laugh and clap Angela's performance. Meanwhile, on went the filming.

But my sister was in earnest. The crowd sensed this and grew quiet. Fortunately Old Strummer came across and took charge. The boys admitted their theft, and Old Strummer marched them across the street and made them buy cakes and biscuits needed for the Freeman shopping basket. So Angela got her own back and the film producer put a pound note in the cap. He said that the film might have to be cut a bit, but that Old Strummer and

Angela would certainly appear in his programme on *New Towns*. Everyone congratulated them; it was certainly a wonderful effort on Angela's part!

Angela was so excited by all this that she ran straight home to tell us about it. But she arrived without the shopping basket which she had left under the sacking in Old Strummer's handcart. It was now past one o'clock and, to start with, my mother was much more concerned about the family shopping than about Angela's triumph. But then Old Strummer, who knew where we lived, turned up and all was well. He was so pleased with the day's takings and with Angela that he insisted on treating us all to fish and chips then and there.

Once again I was proud of my sister. But I cannot help wishing it had been John Freeman out there in the street yesterday!

1. Reading for Meaning

(a) Explain exactly what John means by, *she stood within reach of the enemy*.

(b) Explain, *the film might have to be cut*.

(c) What is meant by, *Old Strummer marched them across the street*?

(d) What made Angela forget to take home her shopping basket?

(e) How was it that Old Strummer was so pleased with the day's takings?

(f) How was Angela's triumph celebrated?

(g) By what means did Old Strummer carry round his ancient piano?

(h) Explain, *he insisted on treating us then and there*.

(i) Suggest another title for this Chapter.

(j) Give the meaning of: *pounced, congratulate, admit*.

H

2. Detective Reading and Discussion

(a) What do you think were the actual words exchanged between Old Strummer and the two boys?

(b) In what ways would the crowd *congratulate* Angela and Old Strummer?

(c) Why was Mrs Freeman more concerned about the missing shopping basket than about Angela's triumph?

(d) What is the meaning of, *the crowd thought it all part of the act*?

(e) What was the film unit doing in Summervale yesterday?

(f) How do you know that John was a little envious of his sister?

(g) What cuts do you think might be necessary in yesterday's film of Summervale?

(h) On what other occasion was John Freeman proud of his sister? (Refer to Chapter 7, p. 47, if you cannot remember.)

3. Reading for Pleasure

Read this passage by Richard Jefferies from *Just Before Winter*.

A rich tint of russet deepened on the forest top, and seemed to sink day by day deeper into the foliage like a stain; riper and riper it grew, as an apple colours. Broad acres these of the last crop, the crop of leaves. A warm red lies on the hillside above the woods, as if the red dawn stayed there through the day; it is the heath and heather seeds; and higher still, a pale yellow fills the larches. The whole of the great hill glows with colour under the short hours of the October sun.

FOR DISCUSSION

(a) Notice the comparison, . . . *like a stain*, and . . . *as an apple colours*, and discuss how the use of comparisons like this helps vivid writing.

(b) What is the meaning of, *a tint of russet*?

(c) What colours are named to describe this autumn scene?

(d) Discuss any particular words, groups of words and sentences which in your opinion help to make this writing vivid and full of imagination.

4. Looking at Words

Examine these four sentences:

There was a film unit <u>recording</u> a programme.

It was followed by the playing of a <u>record</u>.

I can <u>record</u> an accurate account in my diary.

The runner beat the world <u>record</u>.

Explain the meaning of the words underlined.

5. Looking at Verbs: Past and Present

(a) What work does a verb do in a sentence?

(b) Read through Exercise 5 in Chapter 15 which explains the Predicate Word.

(c) Look at the following sentences:

Edgar <u>jumps</u> out of bed. Edgar <u>jumped</u> out of bed.

He <u>goes</u> to school. He <u>went</u> to school.

Which verbs underlined above tell of action in the *past* and which tell of action in the *present* time?

VERBS CHANGE THEIR FORM TO SHOW THE PRESENT OR PAST TIME, OR TENSE.

(d) Fill the five blanks in the columns below. Then underline all the ten verbs in your exercise book.

PRESENT TENSE	PAST TENSE
——	Angela brushed her hair.
John rides his bicycle.	——
He eats his food.	——
——	She cleaned her teeth.
Old Strummer plays the piano.	——

(e) What changes would you make to the verbs in the five sentences printed in Exercise 5 (d) on the previous page to make them form the *future* tense?

(f) Rewrite the following, altering the seven verbs into the form needed to change them into the present tense.

> Tom stood still and watched him, while he swelled himself and puffed and stretched himself out stiff. He moved his legs feebly and looked about.

(g) Rewrite the following putting the seven verbs in the past tense:

> As the creature sits in the warm sun, a wonderful change comes over it. It grows strong and firm; lovely colours show on its body; out of its back rise four wings, and its eyes grow large and shine like ten thousand diamonds.

(h) Give the subject words for each of the five sentences printed in Exercise 5 (d) on the previous page.

(i) Write out clear and brief notes for a short lecture on verbs. Give your own examples.

5. Tricky Words

Watch your spelling and write a sentence using each of these verbs in the *past tense*. Each verb must end with the letter **t**.

keep	send	leave	weep	mean
lose	bend	build	feel	spend

6. Dictionary Work

(a) Arrange the words printed in Exercise 5 above in strict alphabetical order.

(b) Look up the meaning of these words in your LITTLE DICTIONARY. Write each of them in a separate sentence:

tense	feeble	producer
predicate	congratulate	meter

A storm at sea

7. Composition Work

(a) Write the opening paragraph for a composition on *The Storm*, using about a dozen vivid sentences. Describe the feeling of clammy heat, the far-off sounds and sights of the approaching storm, and end with the actual downpour.

(b) Read through the section in Chapter 6, Exercise 6, p. 43, on LOOKING AT PARAGRAPHS, and then give an orderly plan for four paragraphs for a composition on *Saved from Drowning*.

(c) Write a composition, based on your own orderly plan for paragraphs, on one of the following four subjects:

A narrow escape.

The day our house caught fire.

Our skiffle-group hits the headlines.

My own story (told by your dog who was lost for three days).

8. Things to Do

Suggest three books for the library at Angela's junior school.

Suggest three poems for reading aloud to a class of eight-year-olds.

Suggest a good story for telling to a five-year-old.

Explain what a *riddle* is and give an example.

Write a letter to the headmaster or headmistress of your school explaining that you are absent because of influenza. Address the envelope.

Suggest a good film for Charlie Hunter's father to see.

Suggest two good hymns to sing at school.

9. Additional Work for those who have time

Choose another composition subject from the list in Exercise 7 (c) on the previous page. Make an orderly plan, then write your composition.

Write down three subjects for a composition.

Lewis Carroll wrote a number of 'nonsense' poems. What else did he write?

Write the opening paragraph for a composition called *Emergency Ward*.

Explain what a *chef* does and why he wears a hat at work

19

A Visit to Grandma

LAST SATURDAY, MR HUNTER lent us his car and we had a day's outing in London. First we went to see Grandma in Camberwell. Her home is not far from where we used to live before we moved to Summervale.

She insisted on fussing over Mother as though she was a small girl. This was because they had not seen each other since the appendix operation last month, and it made me try to imagine them together when Mother was Angela's age.

We arrived at mid-day, earlier than expected, and Grandma had forgotten to put in her false teeth—dentures, as she calls them. Angela and I couldn't help bursting out with laughter. She was quite cross for a moment and then joined in good-naturedly.

It seems Grandma much prefers to live in Camberwell and she told us sternly that she had no time for these new towns and housing estates. It must be something to do with age. All our friends are delighted with Summervale, but Father says old people get attached to the houses and streets they have always known and that they often prefer to stay put, whatever the living conditions are like.

After a tremendous lunch, we all went up to the West End. Father left Mr Hunter's car beside one of those parking meters, and he put a shilling in the slot. This turned out to be a waste of money as it was a Saturday afternoon!

Then we went to a new musical at the Drury Lane Theatre. It was a lovely show with singing, dancing and colourful costumes; we all congratulated Mother on her choice. The part I liked best was a hot jazz number.

Afterwards we took Grandma back to Camberwell and then went to the Lyons near Leicester Square for another splendid meal. Angela felt a bit sick on the way home, but reached Summervale without disgracing herself, thanks to a short stop and walk round the pond on Putney Common. I wish we went to the theatre more often, as it's a bit more alive somehow than films and T.V.

1. Reading for Meaning

(a) Where did the Freemans live before they moved?

(b) Why did Grandma fuss over Mrs Freeman?

(c) Who chose the musical the Freemans saw in London?

(d) What helped to prevent Angela from being sick?

(e) How do you know that parking meters in London are 'free' on Saturday afternoons?

(f) Why did John wish he went more often to the theatre?

(g) Suggest another title for this chapter.

2. Detective Reading and Discussion

(a) Suggest reasons for and against the Freemans' move from Camberwell to the new housing estate at Summervale.

(b) What made Grandma cross with John and Angela?

(c) What is the purpose of parking meters in the centre of a large city like London?

(d) Did Grandma eat with the Freemans near Leicester Square?

(e) What does John mean by writing that Angela reached home *without disgracing herself*?

(f) Discuss John's view that the theatre is more alive than films or T.V.

3. Reading for Pleasure

In 1870 some friends of the Rev. Francis Kilvert visited London. Unlike the Freeman family, they were unable to reach home after their outing and had to stay in London. This is what Kilvert recorded in his diary for Tuesday, 8th February.

Miss Child showed me her clever drawings of horses and told me the adventures of the brown owl 'Ruth' which she took home last year. She and her sister stranded in London at night went to London Bridge Hotel (having missed the last train) with little money and no luggage except the owl in a basket. The owl hooted all night in spite of their putting it up the chimney, before the looking glass, under the bedclothes, and in a circle of lighted candles which they hoped it would mistake for the sun. The owl went on hooting, upset the basket, got out and flew about the room. The chambermaid, almost frightened to death dared not come inside the door. Miss Child asked the waiter to get some mice for 'Ruth' but none could be got.

FOR DISCUSSION

(a) Why did Miss Child and her sister try to make 'Ruth' believe it was daylight?

(b) How can you tell from the passage that, although trains are mentioned, all this happened quite a long time ago?

4. Punctuation: Conversations

Discuss the difference in meaning between these two sentences:

    Jenkins said the driver was in the wrong.

    'Jenkins,' said the driver, 'was in the wrong.'

Notice the use of commas and capital letters in the above sentences. What other punctuation marks are used?

Discuss the punctuation in the following sentences:

Mr Hunter said, 'Would you like to borrow my car?'

'Thank you,' said Mr Freeman, 'it is kind of you.'

NOTICE THAT

A comma separates words actually spoken from the rest of the sentence.

The first word spoken begins with a capital letter.

For a new speaker, start on a new line.

When are inverted commas or quotation marks used?

Punctuate the following sentences, putting in capital letters, commas, full stops and question marks to make their meanings clear. Notice the one comma given in the last example.

If necessary, look back at the punctuation guides in Chapter 2, Exercise 5, p. 18.

One fine day as I was walking home I met Mr Hunter

Is your father at home he asked

Yes I replied he is in the garden

I hear you're taking the family to London said Mr Hunter

Yes answered Mr Freeman we're going to Camberwell

Mr Hunter said then you'll borrow my car, won't you

5. Find four abbreviations among the six sentences above and write each of them in full. How many proper nouns are there in these sentences?

6. Looking at Words

(a) Complete the following sentences by choosing the correct word from the two given in italics:

Mr Hunter dislikes cleaning out the —— in the morning. (*grate, great*.)

We are going to Scotland —— there is beautiful scenery. (*wear, where*.)

The highwayman —— slowly towards the inn. (*road, rode*.)

(b) Give six of your own ideas and associations for each of the following: theatre jazz joke cowboy camel triumph.

7. Composition Work

(a) Write down a plan for paragraphs on the story of your underwater exploration the day you met a shark. (Discuss the apparatus needed for underwater swimming, if necessary.)

(b) Write your exciting story, *Underwater Adventure*, based on your own plan, or,

Write a story on *The day Mr Stinker opened the new science block at Summervale School* based on your own plan for paragraphs.

8. Letter Writing

You have received an invitation to Charlie Hunter's birthday party. Write a letter in reply saying that you are sorry you cannot come as you are going to London with the family that day.

Remember to write your address, the date, etc. (Look back to Exercise 3 in Chapter 11 if necessary.)

Address envelopes to:

Your father   your mother   John Freeman
a friend   your uncle   your headmaster or headmistress

9. Library Work and Research

(a) Name three books you yourself have read which you think *either* John Freeman *or* Angela Freeman would enjoy, and give your reasons.

(b) Name a book or play or poem written by two of the following authors: Charles Dickens William Shakespeare Lewis Carroll Robert Browning Alfred Noyes

(c) Name a famous person, living or dead, connected with each of the following: Music Painting Exploration Sport

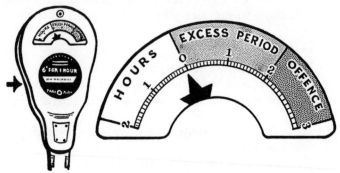

A parking meter

(d) By reference to the above diagrams and by further research, describe how a parking meter works.

(e) Discuss the difference between a magazine and a book.

(f) Find out the rules and regulations governing parking meters

(g) What is the first 'book' in the Bible? What is it about?

(h) Write down the Roman numerals 1, 2, 3, 4, 5.

10. Additional Work for those who have time

Write out one short passage suitable for *Reading for Pleasure* from any book or poem you know.

Suggest the best cure for a heavy cold.

Miss Child's owl was called *Ruth* **(see page 121)**

20

More about Fire

READ AND DISCUSS the following five passages selected
from those which John Freeman and Charlie Hunter collected for the work their form is doing on *Fire Through the
Ages*.

I. Sept. 2nd, 1666. Diary of Samuel Pepys—The Great
Fire of London

It is now burning down all Fish Street, by London
Bridge. So I down to the waterside, and there got a boat,
and through the bridge, and there saw a lamentable fire.
Everybody endeavouring to remove their goods, and
flinging them into the river, or bringing them into boats;
poor people staying in their houses as long as till the
very fire touched them, and then running into boats, or
clambering by one pair of stairs by the waterside to
another; and nobody, to my sight, endeavouring to
quench it, but to remove their goods and leave all to the
fire.

II. From the notebooks of Samuel Butler—Fire

The other night I heard a man say: 'That corner stack is
alight now quite nicely.' People's sympathies seem generally to be with the fire so long as no one is in danger of
being burned.

III. A Camp Fire

A great thing for a cooking fire is to get a good pile of
red hot ashes, and if you use three large logs, they should
be placed lying on the ground, star-shaped, like the

spokes of a wheel, with their ends centred in the fire. A fire made in this way need never go out, for as the logs burn away, you keep pushing them towards the centre of the fire, always making fresh red hot ashes there. This makes a good cooking fire, and one which gives very little flame or smoke.

IV. Forest Fire

'Chang!' he screamed, 'Chang! It is a great elephant herd running for their lives from the fire. They will be upon us in another minute. Run for your lives!' and he plunged into the jungle, followed by the terrified and screaming people.

Savat ran after the crowd. The trees pressed in upon him as he ran in headlong flight. He must hurry faster. Then he tripped and fell. He was just about to spring to his feet when he saw that the elephant herd was upon him. He could not have moved a finger to save his life; he lay there in fear, turned to stone, and saw in a nightmare the avalanche of flying feet of hundreds of elephants as they thundered past, screaming and trumpeting with terror! Their great, dark bodies fanned him as they raced, not three feet away.

V. Fire at the Cable Factory, 1850

A fireman happened to notice the two boys just as they started forward. But although they both heard him shout to them to come back, neither hesitated a moment.

David at least had some protection from Henry's hose. Henry himself, however, had no such help. He met the full heat from the timber fire on his left. He could scarcely see anything. His eyes were smarting and streaming. His lungs were choking with hot, bitter smoke which made his head reel.

Fire at the Cable Factory, 1850

To turn back now was more dangerous than to go forward. Henry struggled towards the steps. There was water enough in the river, and they must reach the ship and save the cable. But first he must reach those steps. Henry dropped down on all-fours and started to crawl forward.

At this moment his friend David, now safe by the steps, turned, expecting to find Henry at his side. Then his whole body stiffened as a gust of wind cleared the smoke from the path for an instant. David saw that Henry had lost all sense of direction. He was crawling straight for that furnace of timber. Straight forward to certain death.

1. Fire Through the Ages

There are many ways in which John Freeman and Charlie Hunter and the rest of the class might have worked on the form project, *Fire Through the Ages*. In fact, the class divided up into groups and after considerable research came together and each group leader made a report. Then the work was put together to make a form magazine, everyone in each group contributing something. You may be able to work on some of the following:

(a) Stirring Fire Stories

Find good stories about some of the following:

The burning of Rome	A volcanic eruption
A legend on the discovery of fire	Guy Fawkes
Fire-fighting	Fire beacons

Give references to books, authors and publishers where possible.

(b) Fire as a Friend and Fire as a Foe

Make two columns with the above as headings, then list below each the ways in which fire can be a 'friend' or a 'foe'.

(c) Fire-fighting

Give an account of either present-day fire-fighting methods or of fire-fighting 100 years ago, or give a comparison between the two.

(d) Safety precautions

Describe briefly some of the safety precautions against fire in each of the following places:

home   school   public buildings   ships   aircraft
mines   railway trains   cinemas

(e) Making fire

List and explain some ways of making fire without using matches.

(f) Draw pictures or make diagrams to illustrate some of the suggestions in (e) above so that they could be included in a form magazine.

(g) Write a newspaper report based on one of the passages

(I, III, IV, V) in this chapter, adding any realistic touches you like. Be sure to report your interview with someone closely concerned, and you may invent names and places if necessary. Add headlines.

(h) Write a short letter to a friend describing how you carry out fire drill at school. Address the envelope.

(i) Give newspaper headlines for a crash at **Summervale Airport**.

2. Understanding English: More Singular and Plural Nouns

(a) Notice how these singular nouns form their plurals:

SINGULAR	PLURAL
piano	pianos
solo	solos
photo	photos

(b) There are other nouns which form plurals in a number of different ways.

First examine and discuss these two groups:

GROUP (I)		GROUP (II)	
lady	ladies	knife	knives
baby	babies	loaf	loaves
fly	flies	leaf	leaves
library	libraries	wife	wives

Now give two general rules to help form the plural of nouns ending in (i) *y* and (ii) *f* or *fe*.

NOTICE THESE EXCEPTIONS

monkey	monkeys	roof	roofs
donkey	donkeys	chief	chiefs
key	keys	dwarf	dwarfs
toy	toys	cliff	cliffs
valley	valleys	safe	safes

(c) Give the plural form of these singular nouns:

dish aeroplane brush coach door penny calf
life head cherry toy army berry chair hair

(d) Notice that some nouns have quite different or exceptional plurals for which there can be no general rule:

tooth	teeth	woman	women
child	children	ox	oxen
sheep	sheep	deer	deer

(e) Give the exceptional plurals of these singular nouns:

foot   **man**   mouse   goose   trout

(f) Make two columns headed SINGULAR and PLURAL and write down the following common nouns in their correct column:

adventure   diary   details   account   events   family

(g) Complete your columns for Exercise (f) above by putting the singular or plural noun in the place of the blank spaces.

3. Things to Do

(a) *Either* draw a picture of *one* of these subjects:

summer   autumn   winter   spring

Then write four lines of poetry under the picture.

Or

Make diagrams showing how *one* of the following works:

a fountain pen   a tap   a pair of scissors
an electric kettle   a safety pin

Then write a short and clear explanation under the diagrams. Give your diagram a title.

(b) In February 1943 a peasant saw a crack open in his cornfield and smoke and ash shoot up from it. Three days later a volcano 550 feet high had been formed.

See if you can find out more about the story of this Paricutin Volcano in Mexico.

(c) Find out the meaning of the following words, then write each one in a sentence. (Use your LITTLE DICTIONARY.)

refugee   slogan   helicopter   mannequin   gendarme

(d) Look up General de Gaulle in your WHO'S WHO.

21

Jour de Fête

NO SPEECH DAY this year, but I'll get my metalwork prize at the end of Assembly on the last day of term. Instead we had a Garden Party just before the Whitsun holiday. Not one of those stuffy affairs organised by adults with children allowed only to run errands. Nothing of the sort! It was a real *jour de Fête*, organised and run by the school, staff included, in proper French style. Apparently it all started in France when twenty seniors went to Paris last Easter. They seem to have been preparing for it ever since! All the money collected is going to help refugees.

The playground was lined with stalls selling soft drinks (prepared by girls at school), paper hats (made by Form 5 in our Art Room), and Paris newspapers. Slogans about General de Gaulle were chalked on blackboards and our headmaster arrived by helicopter on the playing fields. He wore a large sash, decorated in the French national colours. As he stepped out of the helicopter, the Mayor of Summervale drove up in a French car and they kissed each other on both cheeks in true French style. This started the cheering from the enormous crowd of parents and locals and young people.

The Art classes had done all the posters and advertising, and the staff toured Summervale in a loud-speaker van, so everyone turned up in force.

During tea the girls put on a mannequin parade, and

Jour de Fête

three different French plays were given in the hall during
the afternoon. Also we had many exhibitions on travel,
photography, sport, etc. I had a part in *Le Petit Chaperon*

Rouge (Little Red Riding Hood). At the end I cut off the wolf's head with a tremendous flourish and cried, 'maintenant il est mort!' I explained to Angela *before* the play that this means, 'now he is dead'. I spoke out boldly and waited for the curtain to drop. But it didn't! It must have got stuck. But no one minded and everyone cheered. I bowed and walked off the stage.

Then came the bicycle race. This *tour de France* started with a parade led by gendarmes, and the competitors raced three times round the fields, finishing up in the courtyard. The winner received the traditional kiss on both cheeks from the Lady Mayoress. The day ended with the singing of the 'Marseillaise'.

Altogether we collected over £100, and I bet every other school in Summervale wished *they* had thought of the idea first! The money is to help build a home for a refugee family. Perhaps we'll always do something like this instead of Speech Day. I hope so.

1. Reading for Meaning

(a) Why was there no Speech Day at John's school this year?

(b) Where and when did the idea of a *jour de Fête* start?

(c) What is the traditional form of official greeting in France?

(d) What is the meaning of, *everyone turned up in force*?

(e) Why did John have to bow and walk off the stage?

(f) What was the purpose of the *jour de Fête*?

(g) Which things on sale at the stalls were made at school?

(h) When and where will school prizes be given this term at John's school?

(i) In what subject has John done well this term?

(j) What is the name of the French National Anthem?

(k) Suggest another title for this chapter.

2. Detective Reading and Discussion

(a) Is John being unkind and unfair when he writes: *Not one of those stuffy affairs organised by adults*?

(b) How was the *jour de Fête* advertised in Summervale?

(c) What do you know about General de Gaulle?

(d) What are the French national colours?

(e) How do you know that Angela knows no French?

(f) If the Garden Party had been in English style, 'translate' the following:

kissing on both cheeks   gendarmes

Le Petit Chaperon Rouge   Jour de Fête

tour de France   mannequin   Marseillaise

(g) In what other ways can refugees be helped besides sending them money?

(h) Find out the tune of the French National Anthem.

(i) Give some of your own ideas for a school speech day.

(j) What is the difference between a refugee and an orphan?

3. Reading for Pleasure

Read this passage, *Bank Holiday*, from Katherine Mansfield's book, *The Garden Party*.

A stout man with a pink face wears dingy white flannel trousers, a blue coat with a pink handkerchief showing, and a straw hat much too small for him, perched at the back of his head. He plays the guitar. A little chap in white canvas shoes, his face hidden under a felt hat like a broken wing, breathes into a flute; and a tall thin fellow, with bursting over-ripe button boots, draws ribbons— long, twisted, streaming ribbons—of tune out of a fiddle. They stand, unsmiling but not serious, in the broad sun- light opposite the fruit-shop; the pink spider of a hand beats the guitar, the little squat hand, with a brass and turquoise ring, forces the reluctant flute, and the fiddler's arm tries to saw the fiddle in two.

FOR DISCUSSION

Some sentences are unusual and yet particularly effective:

> e.g.   The pink spider of a hand beats the guitar.
>
> The fiddler's arm tries to saw the fiddle in two.

Choose and consider other words, or groups of words and sentences which help to make a vivid and descriptive picture of *Bank Holiday* in Katherine Mansfield's paragraph.

4. Looking at Words

Give half-a-dozen of your own ideas or associations which spring to mind for each of the following:

helicopter   refugee   speech day   France   haystack

5. Letter Writing and Reporting

(a) Imagine you are at school in France. Write a letter to a friend in Summervale describing the day when the French school had an *English Garden Party*. Write your address, making up a name for the French school which is in Rue de Gaulle, Paris 18, France.

(b) Address the envelope for the above letter.

(c) Write a newspaper report on one of the following:

The arrival of the headmaster at Summervale School by helicopter yesterday, and his meeting with the Mayor. (Don't forget to report your interview with the pilot, Mr Mayor and the headmaster.)

The *tour de France* at Summervale School yesterday in which your son and Charlie Hunter fight out an exciting finish. (Don't forget to report your interviews with the winner and, perhaps, with the Lady Mayoress who presented the prize.)

The mannequin parade at Summervale School yesterday. A detailed report of the parade while the audience took tea at small tables under huge colourful umbrellas on the playing fields. (Don't forget to report your interview with the beautiful girl in the latest Paris gown.)

6. Understanding English: Adjectives

(a) Study Exercise 5 in Chapter 11 on common and proper nouns.

(b) Look at the words underlined in this sentence:

> The audience took tea at <u>small</u> tables under <u>huge</u>, <u>colourful</u> umbrellas.

Consider the work that each of these words does in the sentence above: *small*, *huge*, *colourful*. The word *small* describes or tells us something more about the noun tables. The words *huge* and *colourful* describe or tell us something more about the noun umbrellas.

ADJECTIVES TELL US SOMETHING MORE ABOUT (OR QUALIFY) NOUNS.

(c) Find four nouns in the sentence in (b) above and say which is singular and which is plural. (Refer to Chapter 17 if necessary.)

(d) What is the Predicate Word in the sentence in (b) above?

(e) Three adjectives are underlined in the following passage. Find five more adjectives in it:

> The trees were <u>lovely</u>. With their broad, gleaming leaves and their clusters of yellow fruit, they were like trees growing on a desert island, <u>proud</u>, <u>solitary</u>, lifting their leaves and fruit to the sun in a kind of silent splendour.

NOTICE

(i) The adjectives underlined do not come in front of the nouns they qualify. Name the nouns qualified by each of the adjectives underlined.

(ii) More than one adjective can qualify the same noun.

(f) Write a few sentences of description about each of the following, using some of the adjectives supplied with nouns of your own choice.

A CHRISTMAS TREE: tall   green   glittering   silvery
A COWBOY: muscular   sunburnt   swift
SUMMER: hot   blue   sunny

(g) Arrange the following adjectives in order, beginning with the one which means coldest and ending with the one that means hottest:

  tepid   cold   warm   freezing   hot   boiling   frozen

NOTICE:

We call words *nouns* or *adjectives* or *verbs* because of the work they do in sentences. Every word does some kind of work in a sentence. You must always look at the work each word does in its particular sentence:

e.g.   We went for a *swim* (noun).

      We *swim* in the baths (verb).

7. Things to Do and Research Work

(a) See if you can find out something about the automatic sorting of letters which is designed to use postal codes on the last line of the address on envelopes.

Norwich was the first place to experiment with such a scheme. Make notes and report to the class on the results of your research before the end of term.

(b) Find out the date of:

     the next new moon   next Easter

     the next leap year   the next Olympic Games year

(c) List three good places for a summer holiday and prepare a short talk on the advantages of one of them.

(d) List your three favourites: tastes, smells, sights.

(e) In what town and country would you find:

         Nelson's Column   The Eiffel Tower

         The Vatican   The Statue of Liberty

8. Additional Work for those who have time

Describe any *fête* or open-air party or circus which you have seen.

22

Exploring on Bicycles

AT WHITSUN CHARLIE AND I set off towards the East Coast for a few days as we had a week's holiday. We went by bicycle and stayed at Youth Hostels. Charlie did most of the navigation and we explored various villages and roads along the route. We cooked on my new stove which behaved perfectly the whole week.

We had a particularly entertaining time at a Youth Hostel on the way to Aldeburgh. There was quite a gathering of French and German boys and girls, and we had a regular sing-song, also a discussion about schools. It seems that over there much less time is spent on games than in England. It was most amusing when Charlie tried to explain cricket to the rest. We all ended up playing rounders in a nearby field, as the others hadn't any great interest in cricket.

Later that evening we had a riotous time singing French and German and English words all at once to the latest hit tunes until the Warden sent us to bed.

We had a couple of days at Aldeburgh and tried some sailing on the estuary there. The Warden at the local Youth Hostel took us out one afternoon and showed us the ropes. It was much more exciting than I had imagined. What with a fast tide and a gusty wind we had to keep our wits about us all the time. The boat we used had a centre-board, mainsail and jib, and both Charlie and I took a turn at the helm.

On the last day there was a real drama on the beach—nearly a terrible tragedy too. A boy was carried out to sea on one of those rubber mattress things and he was nearly drowned. I'm going to drop a line to Angela and tell her to be careful—bathing in Cornwall is much more dangerous than here.

Carried out to sea

1. Reading for Meaning

(a) What is meant by *navigation*?

(b) What differences did John note between schools on the Continent and his own school?

(c) Who helped Charlie and John to sail?

(d) What is the meaning of *showed us the ropes*?

(e) What do you understand by *a fast tide and a gusty wind*?

(f) What is meant by *take the helm*?

(g) Why did John decide to write to Angela?

(h) Suggest another title for this chapter.

2. Detective Reading and Discussion

(a) Explain the purpose of:

      A Youth Hostel   A centre-board

(b) What songs and tunes might a group of English, German and French boys and girls all know if they met in a Youth Hostel this evening?

(c) Discuss the French boys' view that to play games *every* afternoon at school is ridiculous.

(d) What is an estuary?

(e) What are some of the dangers of sea-bathing?

(f) Is there any good reason why John thinks sea-bathing in Cornwall is more dangerous than on the East Coast?

(g) Consider different ways of life-saving in the water.

3. Looking at Slang

Apart from two special and deliberate uses of slang, John sometimes writes in a way which would not be allowed in a school composition. His style is too conversational, too loose and inexact, and not particularly vivid.

(a) Examine the following and discuss other ways of saying the same thing which would be more correct and accurate for a school composition.

There was quite a gathering.

We had a regular sing-song.

I'm going to drop a line to Angela.

TRY TO AVOID THE USE OF SLANG IN YOUR OWN SPEECH AND WRITING.

(b) Discuss the opinion that books read at school should never contain any slang whatsoever, and that schoolchildren should only read 'pure' English. For example, what would Dickens do with his characters? Would it spoil the 'atmosphere' of conversations? What about Shakespeare?

4. Understanding English: Pronouns

Examine the two groups of sentences below:

(i) Charlie has a bicycle.   Charlie rides a bicycle.

(ii) Charlie has a bicycle.   He rides it.

In (ii) which words are used instead of the nouns, *Charlie* and *bicycle*?

WHEN A WORD IS STANDING INSTEAD OF A NOUN IT IS
CALLED A PRONOUN.

(a) Improve the sentences below by using pronouns:

Angela likes singing and Angela has a lovely voice.

I have two books and the books are at home.

His mother told John his mother was angry.

John said John was sorry.

PRONOUNS, LIKE NOUNS, REFER TO PEOPLE, PLACES
AND THINGS. THEY STAND FOR OR IN PLACE OF
NOUNS.

(b) Notice that you must always consider the work a word is
doing in a sentence before you can decide what part of
speech it is.

e.g.   We went for a *swim*.   (Noun.)

We *swim* in the baths.   (Verb.)

(c) In the following passage ten words are underlined. Five
are pronouns and the other five are either nouns or verbs.
List them under the headings: *pronouns, verbs, nouns*.

When Charlie came to see him on Tuesday he found him
having supper in the kitchen. They then went to his room
and worked there for an hour. After this Charlie left to
help Angela. She was downstairs and he knew where to
find her.

(d) What are the plurals of these pronouns?

I   me   he   him   her   you   she   hers

(e) Use the following pronouns in sentences of your own:

ours   theirs   us   him   you

(f) Make a list of some of the commonest pronouns.

(g) Supply the pronouns for the words repeated in the following sentences:

Charlie said, 'That's Charlie's.'

The hat hangs where the hat was put yesterday.

Charlie and John gave Charlie and John a treat when
they went to the Zoo.

Father called the children and gave the children ices.

Said Angela to her mother, 'No, that dress is not mother's, Angela's has your brooch on it.'

(h) See how many pronouns you can find on page 131.

5. Tricky Words

(a) Make up the sentences to show you know the meanings of each of these words:

tale	weak	write	to	wear	road
tail	week	right	two	were	rode
sent	sale	boy	beach	root	raise
scent	sail	buoy	beech	route	rays
it's	their	peel	steel	sum	
its	there	peal	steal	some	

(b) Pair the following verbs and nouns. When paired they must make sense. Add *the* or *a* as required.

VERBS: bray, is green, ticks, knocked, gobble.

NOUNS: grass, clock, donkeys, turkeys, the postman.

6. Looking at Verbs

(a) Add *is* or *are*:

Charlie and I —— going to the sea.

There —— no paraffin in the primus.

—— Charlie and John ready to sing?

(b) Add *was* or *were*:

Both Charlie and John —— at Aldeburgh.

Angela —— tired.

Eric Hamilton-Smith and John —— friends.

(c) Add *has* or *have*:

John and Charlie —— just had supper.

Some of the food —— been found.

Either the rain or the sun —— helped the crops.

7. To Start You Writing

Write a description of John and Charlie sitting round the camp fire with the others from the Youth Hostel. You can give some of the German and French boys and girls names like Jean, Hans, Annette, Rudolf, etc. With the flickering firelight in their cheerful faces, and the shadows of tall pine trees in the distance against a full moon, you have plenty of material to help you write vividly. PLAN IT IN PARAGRAPHS FIRST!

8. Things to Do

(a) Find out how a primus stove works.

(b) What other stoves are there for use in camping?

(c) Find out what a *jib* is.

(d) Explain what kind of boat each of the following is:
    submarine   punt   collier   launch   barge
    whaler   destroyer   dingy   punt   yacht

(e) Find out what part of a ship each of these is:
    stern   port   hull   prow   bridge

(f) Read the first chapter of *Swallows and Amazons* by Arthur Ransome which is about camping.

(g) List what things you need for a three-day camping holiday.

(h) What is meant by, *to pitch a tent* or *to strike camp*?

(i) Consult *The Hike Book* by Jack Cox (Lutterworth Press).

9. Additional Work for those who have time

(a) From a road map find the distance from:
    London to Aldeburgh.   London to Edinburgh.

(b) Write down the names of:

three daily newspapers	three members of Parliament
three soap powders	three great explorers
three makes of cars	three diseases
three breeds of dogs	three games played with a ball
three capital cities	

23

John sends a Warning

THIS IS THE LETTER which John wrote to his sister, Angela, the day after he saw a boy nearly drowned at Aldeburgh.

Youth Hostel,
Near Aldeburgh,
Whit Monday.

Dear Angela,

Charlie and I leave here tomorrow. We stayed two nights on the way and apart from one puncture, a lost tooth brush and a few arguments, all went well. We had a sail on the estuary—the Warden from the hostel took us out, and I'm planning to do some more during the summer if only I get the chance. Charlie is not so keen, he prefers cricket. How's Cornwall? I hope you're enjoying yourself. You are lucky to have ten days with Auntie May.

You ought to know what happened yesterday. Quite a few people here float around on those rubber mattresses, and a boy drifted out to sea on one. Several men swam after him, but when one of them got into difficulties, the others went to help *him*. Then a local fisherman went out and took the three men safely aboard his boat. Meanwhile the boy on the mattress had to wait ages before the boat was able to reach him. Thank goodness it all ended up all right.

I know you are a good swimmer, but I hope you won't play about on those rubber things. The sea is much rougher in Cornwall, as I found out last year, and in those lonely coves there may not be anyone about with a boat. No doubt you would go in for a spectacular rescue by helicopter or something, but I hope nothing of the sort happens. Anyhow, you have been warned!

I've sent two postcards home and one to Grandma—don't forget to write to her. Remind me to tell you about our session with a crowd of French and Germans in the Youth Hostel.

Give my love to Auntie May and tell her I'm looking forward to the summer holidays.

Love,
John

1. Reading and Writing

(a) John has not put the proper address or the date correctly on his letter. Make up an address and put yesterday's date. Make sure the punctuation is correct.

(b) How do you know that Angela has a longer holiday than John?

(c) Why did the boat take so long to reach the boy on the rubber mattress?

(d) Write Angela's letter in reply to John. Make up an address and date the letter next Sunday.

(e) Write a newspaper report of what happened at Aldeburgh yesterday, complete with headlines. Don't forget your interview with the boy and with the man who went to his rescue and was nearly drowned.

(f) Write a telegram announcing your safe arrival at camp and direct it to your parents at Summervale. (Telephone number, Summervale 4297.)

(g) Discuss the difference between a postcard and a letter, then write a postcard to Grandma in Camberwell from the seaside in Cornwall.

2. Reading for Pleasure

Choose from any book you like one or two paragraphs, or verses of a poem, which appeal to you because you like the way in which they are written. Then copy out the paragraphs, or verses, in your best handwriting and prepare to read them aloud, giving reasons for finding them well-written and interesting. The following books may help you if you cannot think of any for yourself.

Black Beauty	Treasure Island
David Copperfield	Swallows and Amazons
Ballet Shoes	The Eagle of the Ninth
The Book of Narrative Poetry (Laurel and Gold series)	

3. Looking at Proverbs

(a) Discuss the meaning of

Don't count your chickens before they are hatched.

A stitch in time saves nine.

Look before you leap.

These expressions are often used in speech and in writing and we call them proverbs—short, pithy sayings in common use.

(b) Can you think of other proverbs?

(c) Which of the proverbs printed in Exercise 3 (a) above fits this meaning: Action taken as soon as it is necessary saves trouble in the future.

(d) Pair the words in the left-hand column with the words in the right-hand column so that they make a proverb.

Too many cooks	catches the worm
A rolling stone	spoil the broth
The early bird	gathers no moss

4. Like and Unlike

(a) Give words with the same meaning as each of the following:

infant   vast   dress   fight   spill   earnest

(b) Give words with opposite meanings to the following:

courage   hope   prosperity   advance

(c) Find suitable 'as' or 'like' expressions to complete the following:

e.g.   His nose was as ... as a ...

His nose was as red as a beetroot.

He was as brave as a ...   I feel as fit as a ...

It was as heavy as ...   Charlie is as ... as a ...

She was as proud as a ...   Jenkins is as ... as a ...

5. Detective Work

(a) What are these used for?

a stop watch   flour   footlights   bridles   nylon
sledges   a set square   grease-paint   French horns

(b) What is?

Greenwich Mean Time   British Summer Time

(c) Find out how far it is to Aldeburgh from these places:

Edinburgh   Dublin   Manchester   Paris   Berlin

6. To start you Writing

(a) You are about to make your first parachute jump. Write one vivid paragraph describing the scene and how you feel.

(b) You are clinging to a raft at sea after a shipwreck. You have been in this situation for two days when you see a boat coming to your rescue. Describe in one vivid paragraph the scene and your feelings as the boat approaches you.

(c) You have just stopped a runaway horse from bolting into the royal party walking through Windsor Great Park. Describe in one paragraph how the Queen stepped forward and thanked you for your brave action, and your feelings at the time.

Describe fully *either* the most ghastly experience in your life *or* the most wonderful experience in your life. (Four paragraphs allowed, but you must note down your paragraph plan and topic headings first.)

7. Things to Do

(a) Give the authors of the books listed in Exercise 2.

(b) Prepare a list of ten questions to ask a boy from Russia about his school life there.

(c) Describe exactly but very shortly how to do *one* of the following:

mend a puncture   mend a fuse   blow up a balloon
answer the telephone
direct someone from your home to your school

8. Things to Draw

Either draw a sketch map of the route from your home to school, *or* draw a picture for the *Summervale News* on one of the following subjects:

sea-rescue   a rowing race   pony trials
pet's corner   the old salt   tourists

Sea-bathing can be dangerous, even for strong swimmers

24

Holiday Work

AT LAST MY FATHER has agreed to let me take a job during the first part of the summer holidays. This means that I ought to be able to earn enough to cover most of the return train fare to Edinburgh. Charlie and I are planning a bicycle tour in Scotland, staying at Youth Hostels.

Luckily, I knew that Mr Bates might be able to employ me. His own son is working for some advanced exam in French and is spending the rest of this summer in France. So Mr Bates seems quite glad for me to help him on his rounds.

This week I am travelling round in his greengrocer's van, helping with the deliveries. Mr Bates calls at each house to take orders, returning to the van with the householder's basket. He and I then weigh out the fruit and vegetables and I take the basket back to the owner with the bill for payment. While I do this, Mr Bates goes ahead and collects the next basket and order.

I started yesterday and found the weights and measures rather difficult. But so far I've made no mistakes with the change, thank goodness! I know some of the people where we call, and everyone is very pleasant and helpful.

Mr Bates has no shop, he works entirely from his van. He is going to take me up to Covent Garden next week to buy his stocks of fruit and vegetables. That should be interesting, but we have to leave here at 4.0 a.m.!

Yesterday evening Charlie and I started to plan our tour of Scotland. We hope to reach the Isle of Skye and explore the west coast. Everyone says we'll be walking as much as bicycling because of the mountains, but that remains to be seen. Anyhow, I hear that there are splendid Youth Hostels in Scotland—I only hope this glorious weather holds.

1. Reading for Meaning

(a) Why is John particularly anxious to earn money at the moment?

(b) Why can't Mr Bates' son help him on his rounds?

(c) Exactly what does John do on the rounds?

(d) Why is it that John and Charlie may have to do so much walking in Scotland?

(e) How do you know that the weather was fine at the time John wrote this passage in his diary?

(f) Suggest another title for this chapter.

2. Detective Reading and Discussion

(a) Why is Mr Bates' son going to France?

(b) If a customer asked Mr Bates for strawberries yesterday, would he be able to supply them? Give reasons for your answer.

(c) What would you have to pay for:
   1 lb cabbage   2 lb bananas   3 lb cooking apples
   4 lb potatoes?

(d) Why does Mr Bates go to Covent Garden?

(e) Why does Mr Bates leave Summervale at 4.0 a.m. to go to Covent Garden?

(f) Name two towns on the Isle of Skye and the famous and beautiful mountain range there.

(g) Discuss why it is John seems to prefer not to work in his father's shop during this fortnight?

Covent Garden Market

3. Reading for Pleasure

Read this paragraph from *Treasure Island* by R. L. Stevenson in which Jim Hawkins is describing the scene.

> I had crossed a marshy tract full of willows, bulrushes, and odd, outlandish, swampy trees; and I had now come out upon the skirts of an open piece of undulating, sandy country, about a mile long, dotted with a few pine trees, and a great number of contorted trees, not unlike the oak in growth, but pale in the foliage, like willows. On the far side stood one of the hills, with two quaint, craggy peaks, shining vividly in the sun.

FOR DISCUSSION

(a) Consider the meaning of the following without reference to a dictionary:

> a marshy tract   pale in foliage
> the skirts of an open piece of country
> craggy peaks

(b) Notice the descriptive value of certain words like swampy, outlandish, dotted, quaint, vividly.

(c) Find out the meaning of *contorted*.

(d) Find a descriptive paragraph in *Treasure Island* about a person, rather than a scene, and discuss it in detail.

4. Looking at Words

(a) Some words can be more valuable than others in writing. Notice the difference between (i) and (ii) below:

> (i) 'Help! Help!' said Angela.
>   'What's the matter?' said John.
>   'I've twisted my ankle,' said Angela.
>
> (ii) "Help! Help!' yelled Angela.
>   'What's the matter?' shouted John.
>   'I've twisted my ankle,' sobbed Angela.

There are other words you can use instead of *said*, such as:

growled	answered	shrieked	whispered
roared	murmured	cried	sneered

But you have to choose the right word to give it its best and correct value in the sentence you are writing. This is especially important with verbs and adjectives.

(b) Make up sentences using the following verbs with their best value:

snarled	giggled	pleaded	inquired
shrieked	cried	whispered	sneered

(c) Fill the gaps in the sentences below by using one of these verbs: swoops   perches   skim   soars   flutter

The swallows —— across the green turf.

The hawk —— down on its prey.

The robin —— on the fork in the garden.

The feathers —— to the ground from the nest.

The eagle ——far up into the air above.

(d) Here are some nouns and verbs used in talking or writing about light. Make up sentences for each of them:

glitters   flashes   blaze   twinkle   glow   flickers

5. Punctuation

(a) Study carefully the punctuation in the sentences printed in Exercise 4 (a).

(b) Punctuate the following:

At last its finished kindly dont ask me to sew any more buttons on your dresses blouses or coats you must realise that ive no time to sit about doing your work for you theres the shopping cooking washing up and housework to do besides you are quite old enough now to help me with all these jobs in the house this is the last time i sew for you is that clear

(c) Without giving hard and fast rules, discuss some helpful guides to punctuation for a French girl of fourteen who speaks English quite well but who finds punctuation difficult. Give examples to help her.

6. Letter Writing

(a) Write a letter inviting Angela Freeman to your birthday party. Put your own address and give the date of your own birthday.

(b) Write a letter to Mr Peters of Downside Zoo asking if you may go round the cages with one of the keepers during the holidays.

(c) Write a letter of inquiry in answer to this advertisement in the *Summervale News*.

> FOR SALE
> Skin-diving outfit. Excellent condition. Apply C. Hunter, 28 Fore Street.

(d) Address envelopes to:
> one of your friends; to the publishers of this book (their address can be found in the front); to the head of your school; to the Prime Minister.

7. Story Writing

(a) The French girl mentioned in Exercise 5 (c) has an excellent idea for a story but she is not clear how to set it down. Give her some helpful guides on sentence and paragraph writing and planning.

(b) Go to sleep for 100 years and describe what you see when you wake up.

(c) Write a story on *one* of the following:
> What happened after I drank the yellow liquid which made me invisible.
> The runaway horse.
> The wooden-legged spy.

8. Things to Do

(a) Find out three facts about each of these characters:

Molesworth   Just William   Billy Bunter

Jim Hawkins   Hans Brinker   Jennings

(b) Write an advertisement for the sale of a bicycle.

(c) Look up R. L. Stevenson in your WHO'S WHO.

(d) Find out how long *The Flying Scotsman* takes to reach Edinburgh from London.

(e) Without speaking or writing, demonstrate in dumb show how you sew on a button.

(f) Explain why dogs sometimes hang out their wet tongues.

(g) Make a list of where the fire extinguishers are in your school. Copy down the instructions on a fire extinguisher.

(h) What would you do now if someone's clothing caught fire?

(i) Explain to the French girl you have met recently the rules to follow when crossing a road in England. Would the same rules apply in France?

(j) Learn by heart any one passage in the *Reading for Pleasure* sections in this book.

9. Additional Work for those who have time

(a) Consider those questions in Exercise 7 (c) and 8 above which you have not yet answered and do some of them now.

(b) Find out when and where matches were invented, and by whom.

(c) Write a story called, 'In the Enemy's Hands'.

(d) Write 'the story of my life' by a famous star of the screen or stage.

A fire extinguisher

25

Try Your Skill

ONCE AGAIN THERE is a long gap in John Freeman's diary. It does not start again until after the summer holidays. By way of change, therefore, here is a chapter of questions. Try your skill and see how many you can answer.

Some of the questions (but not all) have references to chapters given after them in italics. *You can refer back to these when you are in difficulties or when you have finished and wish to check your skill.* You must find for yourself the actual page in the chapter quoted.

1. Finding the right name

(a) Name the street where Mr Freeman had his shop. *Chapter 2.*

(b) Name the shop in Summervale which was burnt to the ground. *Chapter 15.*

(c) Name the man who left an adder in a shop in Summervale. *Chapter 9.*

(d) Name two poets who remembered their childhood homes. *Chapters 1 and 2.*

(e) Name the man with whom John took a holiday job. *Chapter 24.*

(f) Does John name Mrs Freeman's doctor in his diary? *Chapter 11.*

(g) Give the name of the person who is in charge at Youth Hostels. *Chapter 23.*

(h) Name the actor who opened the baths in Summervale. *Chapter 14.*

2. How can you tell?

Answer each question, then give an example of your own.

(a) If a word in a sentence is doing the work of a verb? *Chapter* 14.

(b) If a word in a sentence is doing the work of a noun? *Chapter* 11.

(c) If a word in a sentence is doing the work of an adjective? *Chapter* 21.

(d) If a word in a sentence is doing the work of a pronoun? *Chapter* 22.

(e) If a verb in a sentence is in the present tense (or time)? *Chapter* 18.

(f) If a sentence is a question or a command? *Chapter* 5.

3. Looking at Words

(a) Use each of these words correctly in sentences of your own:

reign	rain	their	there	weak	week
its	it's	your	you're	red	read

(b) Fill in the blanks with words *opposite* in meaning to those underlined.

Angela's cheeks are rosy, but John's are ——.

I meet Charlie often, but I —— see Jenkins.

—— be punctual; never be late.

The children were not asleep, they were ——.

(c) Use four of the following in sentences of your own:

doomed to destruction	so beautiful that
the delicate foliage	craggy peaks
gleaming in the sunshine	glides across the floor

(d) Write out these abbreviations in full:

I'll   wouldn't   there's   you'd   you've   isn't   don't
you'll   we've   wasn't   won't   she's   doesn't   I've
I'm   he's   aren't   it's   weren't   we're   shouldn't

4. Punctuate:

(a) As Angela ran home she remembered her basket with meat eggs apples and flour in it

(b) Go home Jenkins its late and I dont like your company

(c) Please may I have my shirt jersey and coat asked John here you are said Mrs Freeman now dont bother me again

5. Letter Writing

(a) Do three of the following:

Write a letter from Angela Freeman to Grandma thanking her for the Christmas present of a wrist watch.

Write a letter to Mr Peters thanking him for showing you round the zoo.

Write a letter to Summervale nursery school in answer to an advertisement for daily help at the mid-day meal there.

Write a letter to your brother describing your seaside adventures in the caves.

(b) Now address envelopes for *all* the letters above.

(c) Address an envelope to yourself at home.

6. Diary Writing

Write your own diary for today describing what has happened on *This most exciting day in my life*. Make up anything you like, but it must be well within the bounds of possibility.

7. Composition

(a) Describe *either* a country scene in the snow *or* a town scene in a thunderstorm *or* a public event at school or in the town or village.

(b) Describe one of the following:

How to make rice pudding.   How to sew on a button.

How to put out a small fire.   How to fill a fountain pen.

How to cross a busy road.   How to call the police.

(c) Write a story on *one* of the following:

Disaster at sea.   Escape.

Discovery.   Jungle Adventure.

The day I fought Jenkins.   Pets.

Myself—nurse on the emergency ward.

Myself—alone on the X bar Z ranch.

Myself—in charge of the secret weapon.

Myself—in charge of my two children at the seaside.

8. Library Work

(a) Who wrote?

David Copperfield	Alice in Wonderland
Heidi	Little Women
Swallows and Amazons	Twelfth Night
Treasure Island	The Lady of Shalott
The Highwayman	The Pied Piper of Hamelin

(b) In which books will you find these characters?

Jim Hawkins	The Mad Hatter	Hans Brinker
The March Girls	Mr Peggotty	Tom Brown

(c) Name:

two volcanos   the date of the Great Plague in London

two saints   the side of the body where the appendix is

the king who ruled after Elizabeth I

the present heir to the throne

the present President of the U.S.A.

one of Aesop's Fables

9. Learn by heart a few lines from one of the *Reading for Pleasure* passages in this book. Then say them aloud clearly and correctly with feeling and expression.

10. Set ten questions on English to test that French girl you met recently. Remember that she is 14 years old and that you want to test her composition work and her *Understanding English*.

11. Describe a job you could do in the holidays so as to earn some money.

12. You have three wishes. Say what they are.

13. You have £5. How would you spend it?

14. Explain the different ways of writing:
    a letter   a postcard   a telegram   an advertisement
Give examples of each.

15. Explain briefly which you would rather explore:
    space   underwater   the jungle   under the ground
Give reasons. Now give a list of clothing and equipment needed to carry out the exploration of your choice.

16. Prepare a short talk on one of the following:
    Nursing   space travel   the Cinema
    dancing   my favourite hobby pets
    books   radio plays   Jazz music
    Travelling on the London to Birmingham Motorway

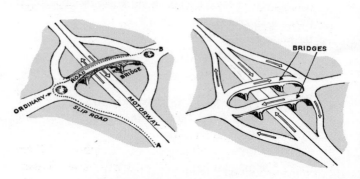

Road junctions on a modern motorway

Who's Who

ALCOTT, Lousia May (1832–1888)

Born in the U.S.A. Was first a teacher, then a journalist. Author of *Little Women* and other famous books for children.

BLAKE, William (1757–1827)

Poet and painter. His best-known verses are *Jerusalem* ('And did those feet in ancient time') and *The Tiger* ('Tiger, tiger burning bright').

BROWNING, Robert (1812–1889)

Born in London. Decided at 17 years of age to be a poet. Married Elizabeth Barret, poetess, in 1846. Author of *The Pied Piper of Hamelin.*

BUTLER, Samuel (1835–1902)

Born in Nottinghamshire. Went to New Zealand and was a successful sheep-farmer. Returned to London and became a writer. Most famous books are *Erewhon* and *The Way of All Flesh.*

CARROLL, Lewis (1832–1898)

Real name Charles Lutwidge Dodgson. Clergyman, Oxford University teacher and mathematician. Author of *Alice in Wonderland* and other stories.

COLERIDGE, Samuel Taylor (1772–1834)

Friend of famous writers and poets, amongst them Charles Lamb, William Wordsworth and Robert Southey. Coleridge himself a fine poet. He wrote *The Rime of the Ancient Mariner.*

DE LA MARE, Walter (1872–1956)

Related to Robert Browning. Novelist and poet. Received two great honours: Companion of Honour and Order of Merit.

DICKENS, Charles (1812–1870)

Famous English novelist. He had a wretched childhood, described in *David Copperfield*. Besides writing novels, he edited various journals and gave public readings from his books. Author of *A Tale of Two Cities*, *Oliver Twist*, etc.

DODGE, Mary (1838–1905)

This writer was left a widow with two young sons and turned to writing to provide for them. Her most famous story is *Hans Brinker or The Silver Skates*.

GAULLE, Charles, General de (1890–   )

Famous French general and statesman, President of the French Republic.

HOOD, Thomas (1799–1845)

Humorous writer, engraver and artist who illustrated his own comic writings. He edited several journals. Best known for the poems *I Remember* and *The Song of the Shirt*.

IRVING, Washington (1783–1859)

Essayist and historian born in New York. Best known for *Rip Van Winkle* and *The Legend of Sleepy Hollow*.

LAWRENCE, David Herbert (1885–1930)

Son of a miner from Nottinghamshire. Was a teacher in Croydon. Then became a poet and novelist.

MENDELSSOHN, Felix Bartholdy (1809–1847)

A German composer. First concert appearance at ten years old playing the piano in Berlin. He travelled all over Europe. He wrote *On Wings of Song*.

NOYES, Alfred (1880–1958)

Born in Wolverhampton. Decided to make his living as a poet. Was for a time Professor of Literature in an American University. Lived in the Isle of Wight. Wrote many poems, among them *The Highwayman.*

PEPYS, Samuel (1633–1703)

Famous diarist. Civil Servant, including the post of Secretary of the Admiralty. Ended his diary, written in cipher or shorthand, when his sight began to fail.

RANSOME, Arthur Michell (1884–   )

Writer of famous books for children. Lives in Suffolk. In 1953 made a C.B.E.

SHAKESPEARE, William (1564–1616)

World-famous poet and playwright. Born at Stratford-on-Avon, where many memorials of him can be seen (his wife, Ann Hathaway's Cottage, etc.). Shakespeare went to London and became an actor and dramatist. Was a shareholder in the Globe Theatre at Southwark in London. He is the greatest English writer of plays. which include *Twelfth Night, Hamlet, A Midsummer Night's Dream,* etc., etc.

STEVENSON, Robert Louis (1850–1894)

Poet, essayist and novelist. Born in Edinburgh. Intended for an engineer like his father and grandfather, but instead became a lawyer. Then became a writer and had a great success with *Treasure Island.* Went to Samoa in 1890 for his health, but died there aged only 44.

TENNYSON, Alfred, Lord (1809–1892)

Poet Laureate of England following Wordsworth. Among his famous poems were *The Lady of Shalott* and *The Charge of the Light Brigade.*

Little Dictionary

The selected meaning given to the words below is that which they have in their context in this book and in the *Little Dictionary* exercises. Many of the words have more than one meaning, and in a few cases a second meaning is given for the sake of clarity. But for the different meanings of all these words, and to find the meanings of words *not* listed here, you must use your complete school dictionary.

Advice	Information or opinion given by one person to another.
Ancient	Very old; belonging to times long past.
Anxiety	Worry and uneasiness.
Apparatus	Equipment or materials needed for performing experiments.
Avoid	To keep away from; to escape.
Barley	Grain used for food or for making malt.
Believer	Someone who trusts or has faith in a person or thing.
Chairman	A person in charge of a meeting.
Chancel	The eastern end of a church where the choir and clergy stand.
Congratulate	To express pleasure and wish joy to someone.
Crisis	Decisive or anxious moment which is a turning point.
Delicate	Fragile, not strong, easily broken or taken ill.

Disqualify	To pronounce someone as unfit and not qualified to do something.
Draper	Shopkeeper dealing in cloth and textiles.
Dwarf	A small person much below the usual size; often met with in fairy tales.
Emigrate	To leave one's homeland in order to settle in another country.
Envious	To be jealous of another person's good fortune.
Experiment	A test or trial.
Feeble	Weak; lacking energy.
Fissure	Thin, deep crack formed when two parts separate.
Flaxen	Pale yellow colour, often referring to hair.
Furrows	Long trenches in the earth made by a plough.
Gendarme	French policeman.
Gondola	Flat-bottomed boat (punt) with high, pointed ends used on canals in Venice.
Helicopter	An aircraft with an overhead propeller which enables it to make a vertical take-off and descent.
Hero	Man admired for his courage, achievements and noble qualities.
Ignorance	Lack of knowledge.
Infectious	Carrying germs of disease.
Jealous	Annoyed by someone else's success; envious and distrustful.
Jumbled	Mixed together, confused.

Lych-gate   Gateway to a churchyard, usually roofed over.

Mannequin   A French word for one who models clothes.
Meter   Machine for measuring
Mingle   To mix or blend together.
Mortar   Cement made of sand, lime and water.

Narrative   An account or story.
Native   (i) Person born in a certain place or country.
                (ii) Belonging to a certain place.

Observe   (i) To watch and notice. (ii) To remark on.
Obstinate   Stubborn and self-willed.
Onlooker   Someone who watches; a spectator.

Precious   Of great price; valuable.
Predicate   That part of a sentence which tells what is said about the subject.
Producer   Someone who organises a play, film or television show.
Programme   A descriptive notice of a series of events.
Pulpit   Raised platform or desk for a preacher.

Quaint   Unusual and odd; old-fashioned.

Ramble   To wander from place to place.
Ranch   Large cattle-farm.
Refugee   Homeless person seeking safety in a foreign land.
Reign   (i) To rule over a country as king or queen.
                (ii) The period of time during which a king or queen rules.

Rhyme   A pairing-off of words that sound alike.

Rhythm   Regular beat or accent that gives basic shape to music; the measured flow of words or phrases.

Russet   Reddish-brown colour.

Saddler   Someone who makes and sells saddles and bridles for horses.

Sanctuary   (i) A place of safety. (ii) A holy, sacred place.

Slogan   Popular phrase used as a motto or for advertising.

Solo   Song or piece of music sung or played by one person.

Steer   (i) A young ox. (ii) To guide a ship or vehicle.

Swell   To grow bigger or louder.

Tense   (i) The form taken by a verb to show whether it is past, present, or future.
(ii) Stretched tightly.
(iii) Nervous, strained.

Tint   A shade of colour, usually light.

Tour   A journey.

Tragic   Very sad, disastrous.

Trough   A long, narrow container for feeding animals.

Tunic   A short coat or dress.

Vivid   Very bright; life-like

Vowel   Any one of the letters *a, e, i, o, u.*

Weary   Tired

Index